A small contribution
Fulham Families. This is to
acknowledge your appreciation,
during your period with the
Team.

Take care
Marie   01/2022

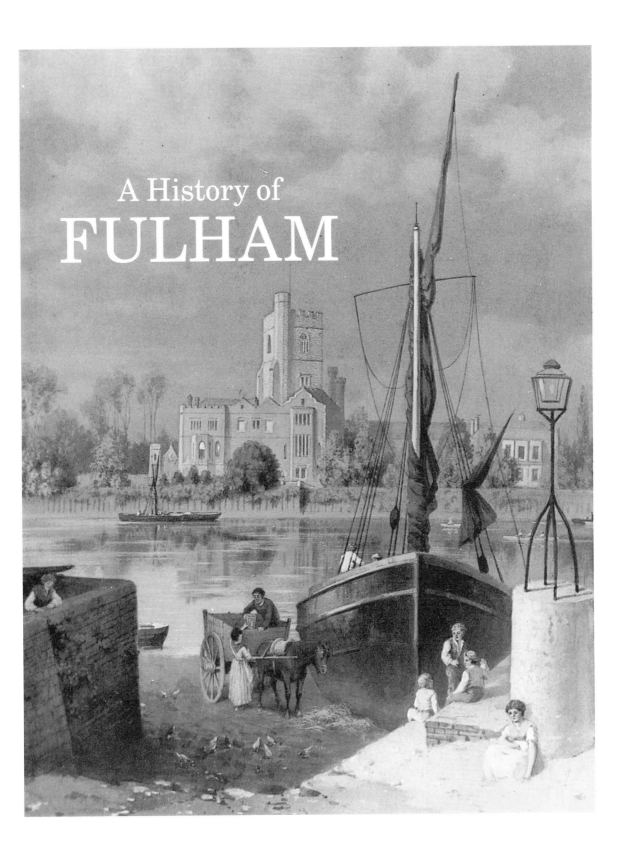

A History of
FULHAM

First published 1990
by Historical Publications Ltd
32 Ellington Street, London, N7 8PL
(Telephone 071–607 1628)

ISBN 0 948667 07 9

Typeset by Historical Publications Ltd
and Fakenham Photosetting Ltd
Printed in Great Britain by
Billings and Company

A History of
FULHAM

Barbara Denny

HISTORICAL PUBLICATIONS

A copy of Verses relating to the parish of Fulham composed by John Sadler, Beadle and Bellman, 1820.

Contents

To my late mother
Beatrice Roberts
1896–1988

ACKNOWLEDGEMENTS

In writing this book I have received generous assistance from many people but I owe special debts to the following: Christine Bayliss, Local History Librarian of the London Borough of Hammersmith and Fulham; the staff of the Clem Attlee Court branch library; Dennis Haselgrove of the Fulham and Hammersmith History Society, for his expert assistance with the chapter on *Church and Churchmen*; Keith Whitehouse of the Fulham Archaeological Rescue Group; Mr H.W. Stroud of Stroud, Nullis and Partners, architects, for information on their restoration of Fulham House; Tony Brown, Senior Public Relations Officer, British Gas (North Thames); David Salsbury of Fulham Pottery; the Marquess of Northampton; Mrs J.R.S. Olivier, headmistress of Lady Margaret School; Michael Thomas, headmaster of All Saints Church of England Primary School; St Thomas Roman Catholic School; D.P. Woolf of Romulus Construction Ltd, for material on Sandford Manor. Last, but not least, I should like to thank my publisher and editor, John Richardson, and my husband, Philip Denny, for his patience and encouragement.

THE ILLUSTRATIONS

Almost all the illustrations have been reproduced by kind permission of the London Borough of Hammersmith and Fulham. The exceptions are the following:
Greater London Record Office, *5, 7, 41*
Guildhall Library, London, *25, 58, 59, 101*
London Transport Museum, *116, 117, 118, 121*
National Monuments Record, *96, 98*
National Portrait Gallery, *52*
The Author and Historical Publications Ltd, *1, 9, 12, 17, 23, 26, 27, 28, 29, 30, 31, 57, 60, 78, 84, 89, 90, 91, 92, 95, 97, 99, 106, 120*

The jacket illustration, of a view of Fulham Church from the Bridge, is repeated on page 10. It was supplied by the London Borough of Hammersmith and Fulham.

The half-title page shows a view of Fulham from Putney, with Pryors Bank in front of Fulham church.

Introduction

So many changes are occurring in present-day Fulham, where I have lived all my life. As it became either convenient or fashionable to move here, and as Chelsea proved too expensive, so Fulham was taken seriously as a suburb once more. Its houses, mostly in pleasant, but architecturally ordinary, terraces were restored and improved to a condition they had never previously aspired to.

At the same time, large areas of Fulham, grimy with the dirt of commercial and industrial undertakings long-established, became derelict. These lands were seized upon for new housing and offices and they were developments no less large than those of the post-war era local authority estates.

To a large degree the present population has no roots in the old Fulham, and I hope that this book will make many curious about its origins, development and vicissitudes. In my experience, people interested in an area's past usually respond by looking to its future. Fulham, like many urban parts of London, threatened by development, excessive traffic and pollution, needs people to care for it. If this book encourages them, I shall be very pleased.

Barbara Denny
1990

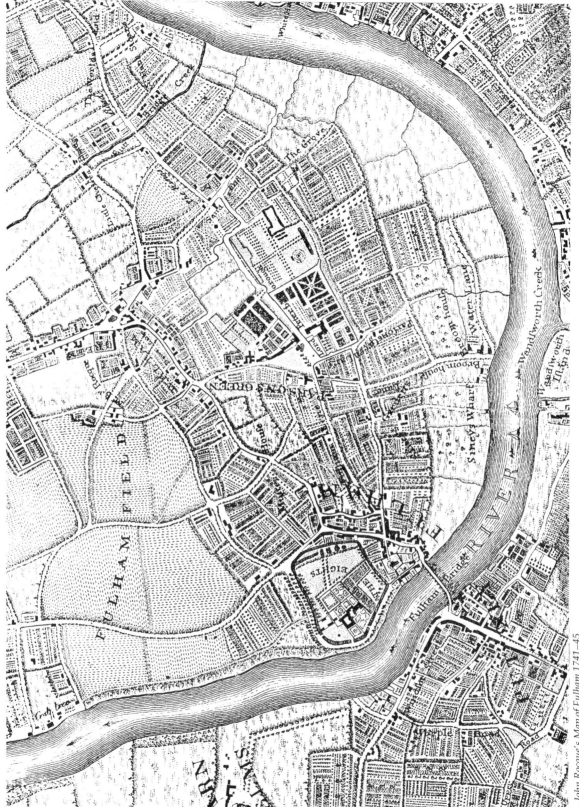

1. *John Rocque's Map of Fulham 1741–45*

CHAPTER ONE
The Old Town

The approach to Fulham over Putney Bridge is a rare London sight for, with a little imagination, this Thames crossing can be seen, in part, as it was a century or more earlier. To the left is the four square tower of All Saints church against a background of trees in Bishops Park, repaired but much the same as it appears in 18th-century prints. In the churchyard are time-worn gravestones and monuments mossy with years, that rise from long grass, ivy-roped hollies and sombre avenues of conifers, and the rooks abuse intruders from the branches of venerable trees. In reality, of course, much has changed. Gone are many old riverside buildings, inns and malthouses and even the bridge was rebuilt 1882–6 about a hundred yards upstream from its old line.

The original 18th-century bridge was of wood, with built-out bays to facilitate the passing of carriages. The high street of Fulham was narrow, lined with shops and cottages without front gardens: much of this went on the realignment of the road to meet the new bridge. In 1906 the road was widened on the western side to accommodate the new tramway, and in the 1930s a further slice was taken off the church garden so as to widen the bridge once more.

Church Gate, which extends from the south-west corner of the High Street to the entrance of the churchyard, is an old and interesting byway. With the exception of nos. 5 and 6, two 17th-century houses which survive, the terrace has been rebuilt. But the almshouses next to it, dating from 1869, have an old enough appearance to recall the 18th-century historian John Bowack's much earlier comment that 'upon the passage leading to the church…are several very handsome houses…'[1], although, of course, he was referring to the tall and elegant dwellings of the day rather than to these cottage-like homes. Church Gate, or Church Row as it was previously called, existed here more than 500 years ago when the old vicarage stood on the south side with an uninterrupted view of the Palace.

Opposite the vicarage was a garden, the site of which was later used for the rebuilding of the William Powell Almshouses. In 1392 Bishop Nicholas Braybrooke granted the garden, then known as Goodyears, to a John Hunt with the stipulation that a passage twelve feet wide should be preserved for the use of himself and his successors.[2] At a manor court in 1561, when the land was referred to as Godeyereshayll, it was ordered that no one should dig soil in the ways leading to the church under pain of a penalty of twenty shillings. Nearby, an open ditch ran down the High Street. This had to be crossed by a bridge, the subject of many admonitions to repair in the court rolls over the centuries; in 1642 this task cost eight shillings.

On Sundays the way was barred to carts and horses; this allowed the church congregation to worship in peace. This could not always have been observed since a Vestry meeting in April 1656 was informed that this traffic 'had been of late very offensive and dangerous to ye people as they have been coming from the church in that narrow passage'. Later, in 1666, it was ordered that a lock and posts should be erected to prevent carts, coaches and carriages from 'spoiling and breaking up the pavement'. When, in the 19th century, the ditch was filled in, the bridge was made redundant. In August 1894, when workmen were excavating a trench in Church Row, a wall of Kentish ragstone,

2. *(Opposite top) A View of Fulham Church from the Bridge. This view, which is reproduced on the jacket of this book, is undated but probably c1740–60. Note the bays in which pedestrians could shelter while vehicles passed.*

3. *(Opposite bottom) Fulham Bridge c1734–48. Oil by Joseph Nicholls.*

4. *Fulham Bridge 1796. Engraved by J. Walker from a drawing by E. Dayes.*

5. *Garden of 7 Church Gate in 1962.*

6. Fulham Vicarage in Church Row.

7. The William Powell Almshouses, 1962.

the same as that used in the old church tower, was found; this was believed to be one of the abutments of the old bridge.

A Fulham vicarage is recorded in the Court Rolls as early as 1430 and in 1658 it is stated that the 'Viccaridge' house with orchards and garden was worth £16 per annum. Originally it was a four-roomed cottage for the ill-paid vicar who, though caring for the souls of the parish, was of slight social importance compared to the rector, who usually held *his* post as a sinecure and derived most of the tithe income. This cottage home was rebuilt in 1750 and Victorian vicars extended it so that when the High Street was widened in 1906 it was so near the roadway and its noise the newly-appointed incumbent declined to use it. He got his way. A new vicarage was built off Fulham High Street and the borough council bought the old site for an open space known now as Vicarage Gardens.

The William Powell Almshouses are on land which has a long history. From 1392 there are records of various owners, cottages and houses, some of which in Tudor times were occupied by the King's Sergeant-at-Arms and wealthy London merchants. In 1696 the land was sold to one, William Skelton,[3] who is said to have owed his position in life to a single incident when, as a footboy to the Bishop of London, Henry Compton, he discovered that the household cook had mixed poison in some broth destined for the Bishop's table. The cook, who had hoped to inherit a small legacy from the Bishop rather earlier than he would normally have done, was dismissed and Skelton was rewarded by being articled to an attorney and appointed subsequently as Bishop's Registrar; in this capacity he was partly responsible for increasing the peal in the parish church from six bells to eight, and his name is engraved on two of them. In 1729 Skelton lost his dog, a domestic drama which is recorded for posterity in an advertisement in *The Craftsman* that year offering a reward of three guineas for its return and no questions asked (dog-stealing was a prevalent crime). The missing pet was described as a liver-coloured and white pointer, very nimble, who had his owner's name engraved on a brass plate on the leather strap around its neck.

Skelton left his Fulham house, by then handsomely rebuilt, to his son, another William. Later occupants were the Batsford family, two daughters of which ran a successful seminary for young gentlemen here. On the retirement of the surviving sister the house went up for sale and Bishop Charles Blomfield, hearing that it was likely to become a private lunatic asylum, bought it himself. The house was demolished in 1843 and the Bishop gave part of the site to extend the overflowing churchyard and the remainder was allowed to the vicar for use as a herb garden. When Blomfield died and the site became the property of the Ecclesiastical Commissioners, the trustees of the Sir William Powell Almshouses in Burlington Road, buildings which were then very dilapidated, obtained the site and on it built the present row of twelve Gothic cottages. These little houses with their pretty front gardens still present an old world exterior despite recent modernisation. The heads of Faith, Hope and Charity are sculpted in their small tower, together with full length figures of Miriam, Anna, Deborah, Dorcas, Ruth and St Mary.

Another resident of Church Row in the early 18th century was the barber-surgeon Robert Limpany, whose family had long been resident in Fulham – in 1579 his namesake had been appointed parish constable. He lived at 6 Church Row, one of the two surviving 17th-century houses, and the arched iron gateway still bears his monogram. Limpany was a great benefactor to All Saints church, contributing generously to the repairs of 1686. John Bowack, his contemporary, noted that Limpany's estate was considerable and that he was commonly called 'Lord of Fulham'. Certainly at one time his property was extensive, consisting of most of Church Row as well as many properties in the High Street including the King's Arms. He lived to the great age of 94 and his

8. Church Row in c1865.

will included a bequest of twenty shillings to the Fulham organist 'so long as the organ shall be used and played upon in the parish church'. Other bequests included forty shillings to purchase threepenny loaves of bread for distribution to the poor in January each year, twenty shillings a year to keep his own monument in the church in good repair, and ten shillings annually to be distributed in 'wigs', a kind of bun, and ale on March 1st to poor children at the charity school, plus three pounds for meat and drink at Christmas. Limpany spent his last days at Church Row, although he had earlier bought another estate on the north side of Fulham Road near the Fulham Palace Road junction, known as Holcrofts, where he had built himself a house of that name.

Better known, but not during his lifetime, was Joseph Roe, House Steward to Bishop Beilby Porteous, whose records, diaries and account books survive to reveal life in the episcopal household in the early 19th century; they include a macabre account of the Bishop's last days and his fear of being buried alive. On 1 May 1808 Roe noted that the Master of the Boys of the Chapel Royal had just died and he was sure the post was in the gift of the Bishop and would go to whoever was willing to pay for it as a sinecure. After all, he remarks, he could not have been himself Sergeant of the King's Chapel unless he had paid the Bishop £1,000 for it. On more commonplace matters he notes some of the alterations he made at his home at 7 Church Row, and the trees and shrubs he bought for his garden. On Sunday, 29 September 1811, after attending church, he went into the garden and 'God forgive me – weeded my cabbages and green cale which was nearly smothered with insects. I also pulled a quantity of Jerusalem artichokes which I presume had been planted for the appearance of shrubs'.[4]

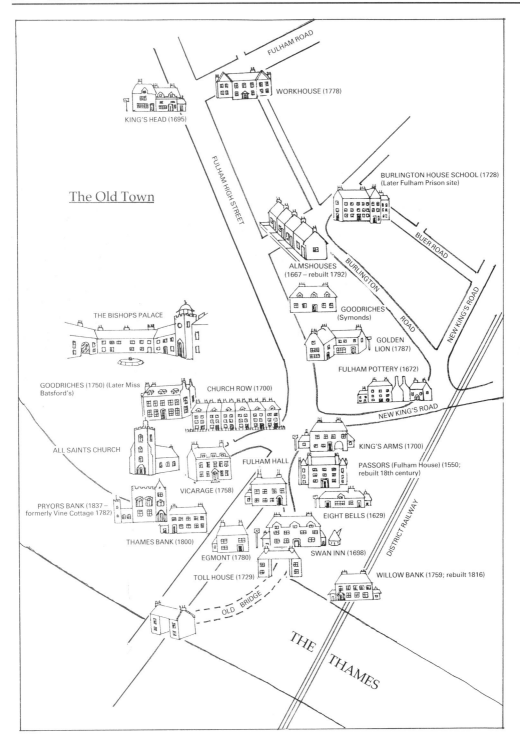

KING'S HEAD (1695)

FULHAM ROAD

WORKHOUSE (1778)

The Old Town

FULHAM HIGH STREET

BURLINGTON HOUSE SCHOOL (1728)
(Later Fulham Prison site)

BUER ROAD

ALMSHOUSES
(1667 – rebuilt 1792)

BURLINGTON ROAD

NEW KING'S ROAD

THE BISHOPS PALACE

GOODRICHES
(Symonds)

GOLDEN
LION (1787)

FULHAM POTTERY (1672)

GOODRICHES (1750) (Later Miss
Batsford's)

CHURCH ROW (1700)

NEW KING'S ROAD

ALL SAINTS CHURCH

KING'S ARMS (1700)

VICARAGE (1758)

FULHAM HALL

PASSORS (Fulham House) (1550;
rebuilt 18th century)

PRYORS BANK (1837 –
formerly Vine Cottage 1782)

EIGHT BELLS (1629)

THAMES BANK (1800)

EGMONT (1780)

SWAN INN (1698)

DISTRICT RAILWAY

TOLL HOUSE (1729)

WILLOW BANK (1759; rebuilt 1816)

OLD   BRIDGE

THE   THAMES

9. *A Sketch map of the Old Town showing many of the features mentioned in this chapter.*

10. The Eight Bells, Fulham High Street, c1880.

Other interesting residents of Church Row included the surgeon Henry Bunnett who vaccinated the workhouse inmates and in whose garden stood, for some inexplicable reason, a statue of a dwarf dressed in a general's uniform. Also here was an eccentric lady called Miss Etherington who shared her home with forty cats.

Stocks and a whipping post stood at the north-eastern corner of the High Street until mid-Victorian times. The first stocks were placed here in 1523 and these were replaced, together with a whipping post seven feet high, in 1667.

Fulham High Street seems an inappropriate name today. It has been superseded as a shopping centre by Fulham Broadway and Putney across the river, but there was a time when this thoroughfare, leading from the ferry which preceded the bridge, to the Bishop's Palace, was the centre of village life. It continued north towards Hammersmith with a fork eastwards on a line now marked by the New King's Road, towards Walham Green and Chelsea. Previously its name was Bear Street, perhaps from an inn of that name or else, more fancifully, a nearby bear pit. Or it might have derived from the Anglo-Saxon *bere* for barley, or *bury* for manor or farm; Charles Fèret, author of the three-volume *Fulham Old and New*, discovered much evidence that it was known as Bury Street in the late 14th century.

An old inn in the High Street is the Eight Bells, now rebuilt on its original site, which, since the re-alignment of the High Street, is in a side road. Its name is assumed to derive from the increase, already referred to, of an additional two bells in the church in 1729; the first mention of this name occurs in the Highway Rate book of 1771, although a Bell alehouse is recorded a century earlier. The Nag's Head occupied the north-west corner of the junction with New King's Road; it is first recorded in the reign of James I, but was closed in the mid 18th century, continuing as private dwellings until demolition in 1895.

11. Passors or Fulham House, Fulham High Street, probably at the end of the last century.

12. Jacob Tonson.

Near the Eight Bells still survives a recently restored, elegant house once called Passors, later Fulham House, named from a family living on the site in the reign of Edward III, a passor being a *passator*, or ferryman. The grounds to the house included a three-acre field known as Passors Mead next to the river. A later occupant was wool merchant Ralph Warren, who was Lord Mayor of London in 1536. The house passed to Sir Thomas Whyte, another Lord Mayor of London, who was also founder of St John's College, Oxford, as well as a benefactor of Merchant Taylors' School. Whyte was instrumental in keeping Londoners loyal to Mary Tudor despite her marriage to Philip of Spain. Son of a poor clothier, he was apprenticed as a tailor to a master who left him £100. Subsequently, and allegedly guided by a vision in a dream, he founded St John's College at a spot where two trunks of an elm tree sprang from the same root.

Passors was inherited subsequently by Sir Henry Cromwell, grandfather to Oliver, but recent research has scotched some of the associations with other illustrious residents suggested by Fèret in 1900. He listed Jacob Tonson famous bookseller and publisher of Milton, Dryden and Pope, as an occupant; certainly Tonson acquired Passors in 1720 but he may never have lived there, treating it as an investment. The matter is further complicated by the fact that Jacob had a namesake nephew, who carried on his business, and a great nephew, also named Jacob, one of whom probably bought another Fulham property at North End and was chosen as reeve of the manor in 1724. Two children of Jacob and Mary Tonson appear in the burial records of the parish in 1726 and 1728. Another member of the family, Richard, took up residence at

Passors in 1761; he demolished four adjacent cottages in 1771 so as to expand the garden.

In 1804 Passors was let to the first of a series of schoolmistresses – the Misses Flemings, who opened the Fulham House School for girls. After them came the Loves, a trio of beautiful women known in their heyday as the 'three graces of Fulham'. For forty years, from 1840, the Misses King ran a similar school.

In 1879 the house was bought by a local builder, Parkins Hammond Jones, whose family continued here until the War Office took it over in 1904 for use as a Territorial Army headquarters. During the First World War it was occupied by the 25th Cyclist Battalion and then by the 7th London Brigade of the Royal Field Artillery, with the troops encamped in nearby Bishops Park; early in the Second World War the front garden was built over, practically obscuring the old facade. A few years ago it seemed that this old property would be demolished, but a campaign by conservationists and local residents influenced the Ministry of Defence to commission its rehabilitation. The restorers discovered an architectural jigsaw as well as much damage caused by vandals. They found outer walls where inner walls might be expected, a change of mind in roof structure, a one-sided staircase instead of a normal, centrally placed one, and cellars and foundations dating probably to the 14th century and possibly earlier. There appears to have been no gas installation at any time – electricity succeeded oil lamps and candles. The original paintwork seems to be on the shutters and scraps of antique wallpapers still cling to parts of the walls.

Sensitive and imaginative restoration was called for, and supplied, and the result has been the recovery of one of the very few remaining treasures of Fulham's past, and something to cherish for the future.

Other houses on this eastern side of the road near the Eight Bells were demolished when the road was realigned to the new bridge. A story is told about one of the inhabitants of these cottages who was known as 'the old coffin woman'. A small, wizened person, regarded by many neighbours as a witch, she occupied an upstairs room of one of the cottages in the early 19th century. She was so obsessed with fear of a pauper's burial that she had a coffin made for her which she kept in her room. Every now and then she had it re-lined and re-oiled which gave it 'the colour of bog oak'. It is even said that she had it fitted with shelves, in the meantime, so that it could be used as a cupboard. When she moved elsewhere the coffin went too and when, due to poverty and infirmity, the workhouse loomed, she refused to go unless she could take her coffin with her. The vicar of the time managed to persuade her that this wouldn't be possible, but promised to store the coffin for her until it was needed. In the 1850s she was duly interred in it.

Still surviving, although not in its original form, is the Golden Lion, rebuilt in 1836. The earlier, Tudor, building had originally been a private dwelling occupied by a family called Wyndout before it became a coffee house and a hostelry. The stories about this ancient inn have been the subject of a scholarly investigation, which has dismissed many of them, but replaced them with facts of equal interest.[5] Most interesting was the account in Fèret that in an apartment off the hall was a trapdoor, from which stone steps led to a vaulted cellar where an archway opened to a further staircase. The vault had not been used for many years and was known as 'Bishop Bonner's dungeon', linking it with the notorious Bishop of London at the time of Mary Tudor, who held many Protestants captive in his palace and had them whipped and tortured to recant their beliefs. When the house was demolished, this passage was explored by a waterman called Joe Hatch who found an implement resembling a grid iron. There was also said to be a number of human skeletons hidden in recesses of the passage, all of which crumbled away on touch. The link with Bonner is supported by the suggestion that the house was once the home of the Bishop's

13. Fulham from Putney, c1883.

mother, Elizabeth Ffrodsham Bonner. The potter John Dwight also lived here for a time when he first came to Fulham in the 1670s.

The old Fulham Volunteers used to keep their arms and accoutrêments at the Golden Lion and it was here, too, that the vestry sometimes held a dinner at the conclusion of the annual Perambulation of the Bounds of the parish.

Near the Golden Lion, probably on the site of the present nos. 49–55, in the mid–18th century, there was a carpet and tapestry manufactory. Its founder, Peter Parisot, is variously known as a commercial adventurer, a spendthrift and a disguised Capuchin priest. The historian Thomas Faulkner, describing Parisot's venture, says: 'About the year 1753 an establishment for the manufacture of carpets was established at Fulham where both the work of the Gobelins and the art of dyeing scarlet and black, as practised at Chaillot and Sedan, were carried on.' Parisot had engaged some workmen at Chaillot whom he first employed at Paddington, but afterwards removed to Fulham where the Gobelin manufacture had already been established and 'where he had conveniences for a great number of artists of both sexes and for as such young persons as might be sent to learn the arts of drawing, weaving, dyeing and other branches of the work.'[6] From this it would appear that Parisot had ideas similar to those of modern youth training schemes, but it has also been suggested that he was, instead, intent on having cheap labour. In his own correspondence and advertising Parisot spoke of setting up an academy of drawing and painting in the hope of attracting government assistance. This was to augment the patronage of the Duke of Cumberland, the least popular of the sons of George III, who was actually generous in both financial support and interest and often visited the works. Parisot himself spoke of his new academy as 'offering employment to both sexes to the weakly as well as the robust' and 'Affording help to many families of the better sort who are burdened with numerous offspring'.[7] More precisely, he stated that 'No apprentices or young persons…will be received but such as are natural born subjects of His Majesty and they will be educated in the Protestant religion.'

Whether Parisot was a benefactor to the young unemployed of the day, or to Huguenot refugees, is a matter for conjecture, for a letter written by an Italian, Guiseppe Baretti, to his brother said the name Parisot was an alias for an anti-Jesuit priest, Father Norbett, who had been allowed by Pope Benedict XIV, also an anti-Jesuit, to seek refuge in Britain provided he carried out work as a missionary. Baretti accuses Parisot of squandering money subscribed to set up his factory 'which might have provided him with an honest livelihood had he exercised the least economy…but he was spendthrift and possessed some eminent qualities, particularly those two cardinal virtues known by the name of incontinence and vanity.'[8] Parisot left Fulham for Devon in 1756 and all his stock was sold at auction, the top price being £64 for a 'magnificent large carpet 18 feet by 13 feet of a most elegant and beautiful design'.[9] The factory was turned into a school and eventually demolished.

In Midsummer 1861 the then Bishop of London, Archibald Tait, later to become Archbishop of Canterbury, laid the foundation stone of the new Fulham National Schools on the site of another old house in the High Street, called Goodriches. This is the confusing namesake of another house in Church Row – a duplication which resulted from the fact that an occupant in the High Street, James Vickers, a City Alderman, had a son who had the other house in Church Row and who called it by the same name.[10] Vickers senior left £1800 in his will to his younger son William provided that at his 'coming out time…he hath the report of his masters to be a good husband and no waster…but if he happen to be a prodigal and a spendthrift' the legacy was to be reduced to £1300. Indeed, Vickers seems to have been beset by worries about his children. Eight years before making his will he had seen his daughter married to a 'wicked and ungodly wretch' who had since deserted her. His eldest son 'having behaved himself very prodigally stubborn so that the University could not endure him' had been sent to Russia on his father's business, married without his father's consent and then returned with his wife and children to beg financial help. Vickers instructed that he was 'to get nothing more than £100 and an excuse for his past deeds having already had four thousand off his father'.[11]

A much later resident of Goodriches in the High Street was Richard Rawlingson, the collector of the Rawlinson MSS in the Bodleian Library at Oxford, and a distinguished topographical antiquary, whose works included *The English Topographer*, (1720).

After use as a school Goodriches was pulled down in 1794 and its site used for a garden.

Four houses which stood nearby formed a portion of the property left by Sir William Powell, a Fulham benefactor of the 17th century, to maintain the almshouses which bear his name; these were demolished in 1895. Out of the rents and profits of his Trust he directed that each year six poor men of the parish should be provided with coats and breeches.

Where Rigault Road now enters Fulham High Street was Marshall's Alley; this derived its name from a Mrs Marshall who kept a greengrocer's shop at no. 35 High Street. The alley, just over three feet wide and passing under no. 37, was removed in 1898 when the present road was built.

The old parish workhouse, built in 1775–76, occupied the site of the shops between Rigault Road and the Fulham Road junction and succeeded other poor houses set up in rented cottages on the same site. Until the end of the 17th

14. *Fulham Workhouse in Fulham High Street, a drawing from memory by C. Wilcox in 1897.*

century the necessities of the casual poor were met by disbursements from the parish Overseers of the Poor: the parish records contain many entries relating to doles for the sick, lame, poor, aged and penniless travellers. Later, the Overseers kept records of the 'pension poor' – those who were permanent residents but who were unable to support themselves. With the growth of such a category the 'out pension' system became cumbrous and in 1731 the Vestry set up a scheme to rent buildings in Bear Street (High Street) 'to serve the purpose of a poor house'. The initial sum of £300 was found from a debt to the parish and on 13 July 1732 the Vestry appointed a Board of Trustees to manage the new workhouse. The inmates were to be 'such poor folk as had the right and were in want of parish assistance to be fed, lodged and clothed'. All such poor 'who had their health and limbs were to be appointed to such work as they were fit for and such proper tools and implements as were necessary to be provided'. No separate pensions were allowed. At the rear of the building was a fruit garden and the 1737 record shows that the churchwardens were able to sell walnuts and mulberries from it to raise over £2.[12]

The workhouse was soon so full that some paupers had to be housed outside. The cost of providing this must have alarmed the Vestry, for in 1754 it employed a new Master who offered his services free, provided that he enjoyed the labour of the inmates. The new Master, a Mr Atlee, in fact sent many of his poor to be employed in the nearby Parisot factory, where they wound silk from six in the morning to six in the evening during the summer, and in the winter only from daylight, with one hour for dinner and half an hour for breakfast.

On the other hand Mr Atlee undertook to have the children taught and instructed in the principles of religion, and ensured that they attended church twice on Sundays. He would also take particular care of the sick and the orders of the apothecary would be strictly observed. He added that the house and its inmates would be kept clean, the children washed and combed each day, and time allowed the inmates to clean and mend their linen. Meals would be served at the proper time and in a decent manner with nothing wasted or wanted.

Mr. Atlee's regime was shortlived. Only five months later, in April 1755, the Vestry ordered that 'In consideration that Mr Atlee has not performed or complied with his proposals and contract with the parish that the churchwardens give him ten days' notice to quit'. The inmates, however, continued at their silk-winding with a one-hour reduction of their summer working hours, and the new Master was recorded as being diligent in seeking out apprenticeships for the children.[13]

The earliest extant workhouse book begins in August 1771 when there were seven men, twelve women and 19 children in a substantial two-storey building, enclosed by a wall, facing the High Street. The front door opened to a central hall and stairs leading to the upper floors. At the rear was a yard in which inmates could take their limited leisure.

The Overseers' accounts for 1785 note the purchase of four new spinning wheels and in 1787 the Vestry considered proposals from Messrs Kilner & Co. for employing inmates in picking and cleaning cotton, but came to the conclusion that unless the firm paid £50 in return for this they would do better to employ the old people in some other manner. Harsh though conditions probably were there are some acts of humanity recorded. In January 1788, William Atkyns, an orphan, was put out for a month's trial to a music teacher so that he could receive violin lessons; the teacher reported that the boy had talent and that in a reasonable time could earn a living from it. He was provided with an instrument and further lessons at twelve shillings for ten periods.

By 1790 the employment of inmates had changed slightly to that of spinning and carding of mop yarn. This was still being spun here into the 19th century but Faulkner observed that a new scheme had been entered into with two businessmen being allowed to erect machinery for cotton spinning in part of the house, for which the parish would receive £50 per year. However, Faulkner remarked, 'it seems doubtful whether it will succeed as there are very few men in the house capable of labour'.[14] During the last years of its existence the only work done by the workhouse inmates was the making of 'strawberry pottles', which were always needed in the nearby market gardens.

At this period the inmates' diet was reasonable for the time – meat four days a week, porridge on five days and bread and cheese on others. In 1802, Dr. William Sharp, a local physician, persuaded the Vestry to provide inoculation against smallpox for the poor of the parish, and Dr. Henry Bunnett, who for many years was 'surgeon apothecary and midwife' to the workhouse, performed the work.[15]

In common with many other vestries Fulham was dismayed by new Poor Law legislation which brought in unions of parishes to form larger units for poor relief. Fulham's workhouse became redundant when a Fulham Union building was erected in Fulham Palace Road, on the site of the present Charing Cross Hospital. The minutes record that Fulham Vestry gave a substantial dinner for all the more respectable inmates of the old building, including the children, prior to their leaving it in 1850.

There once existed in the Burlington Road area a famous boys' school and a prison. This road was known as Sowgelders Lane in Elizabethan times, an obvious reference to its earlier inhabitants, but it later became known simply as the 'back lane' and it was referred to thus by Sir William Powell when he established his almshouses there in 1667. Powell died, however, without leaving regulations for the administration of his charity and eventually it was transferred to the care of the parish. The almshouses, much dilapidated, were rebuilt in 1792, but the use of old materials by the contractor brought consequential expense in later repairs. As we have seen they were replaced by new buildings in Church Gate in 1868, away from the noxious fumes of the Pottery and removed from the area of a newly-built prison.

By then Burlington Road had gone down in the world from the time when the Fulham Academy, later known as the Burlington House Academy, flourished there. In 1728 Lewis Vaslet, a French schoolmaster, bought here 'a house divided into two dwellings together with a stable under the summer-house'. Here he taught Latin and French – he was the author of several text books of exercises in these languages. Another Frenchman succeeded him, a M. Nicholas Guillibeau, although whether as principal or a tutor is the subject of some debate, as indeed, is the location of the school. One of Guillibeau's pupils was the young Lord Compton, son and heir of the Earl of Northampton, and the Compton family amassed a fascinating collection of letters written by the old schoolmaster and his pupil between 1734 and 1737.[16] The letters are mostly addressed to the Countess, the boy's mother, but her replies, unfortunately, have not survived. In November of 1734 Guillibeau writes to her that 'His Lordship continues in very good health only his hollow tooth has felt a little discomfort these four or five days but since I have stopped the hole with a grain of mastick it has been easier'. Later, the master thanked the Earl and Countess for the 'very fine piece of venison and the rabbits', and subsequently reported that 'His Lordship drinks no malt drink, the beer here being newer than he is used to at home makes him dislike it, so I thought I would mention this to your Ladyship because this is about the time Your Ladyship used to order wine for his Lordship's use…'. When the boy was ill in 1737 Guillibeau wrote to his parents that 'He ordered His Lordship one of Gascoine's Powders every six hours'.

A subsequent owner of the academy was Dr. Robert Roy, who had run a large and successful school in Old Burlington Street, Piccadilly, and it was during his time that the Fulham school received the name of Burlington House.[17] Dr. Laumann, who followed him, advertised that the boys would be 'carefully instructed in the Latin and Greek languages, mathematics and the usual branches of liberal education preparatory to their introduction to the public schools or the Royal Military or East India Colleges. Those pupils who are intended for the Counting Houses are diligently prepared in vulgar fractions, exchange with foreign countries etc.' The house, he claimed, was large and airy and 'each young gentleman has a separate bed'.[18]

The school grounds covered over three acres and these and the house itself were purchased by the government in 1855 for the purpose of erecting a reformatory for women prisoners, called Fulham Refuge. This was built in 1856 on the site of the school cricket field. Its appearance was certainly grim enough, being surrounded by a high wall with a fortress-like gateway surmounted by spikes. The women were trained in laundry work and industrial occupations and usually spent two or three years there. For the younger prisoners there was a school in the prison. Sir Joshua Jebb, in his capacity as Director General of Prisons, took a keen interest in this institution the inmates of which were known as 'Jebb's pets'. After a while the Refuge was converted into an ordinary prison and the building enlarged to accommodate 400 inmates.

The premises occupied three sides of a square, the fourth being the chapel; the cells were arranged in tiers around several blocks, access being gained by staircases leading to the narrow galleries around the floors. In one of these cells, no. 29, Constance Kent was confined for the murder of her little half-brother Francis Saville Kent at Road, Somerset, in 1860, after one of the most sensational murder investigations of the Victorian era. There were also remand

15. Burlington House School, from a litho by C. Hawkins.

16. Fulham Refuge, later Convict Prison, in 1894.

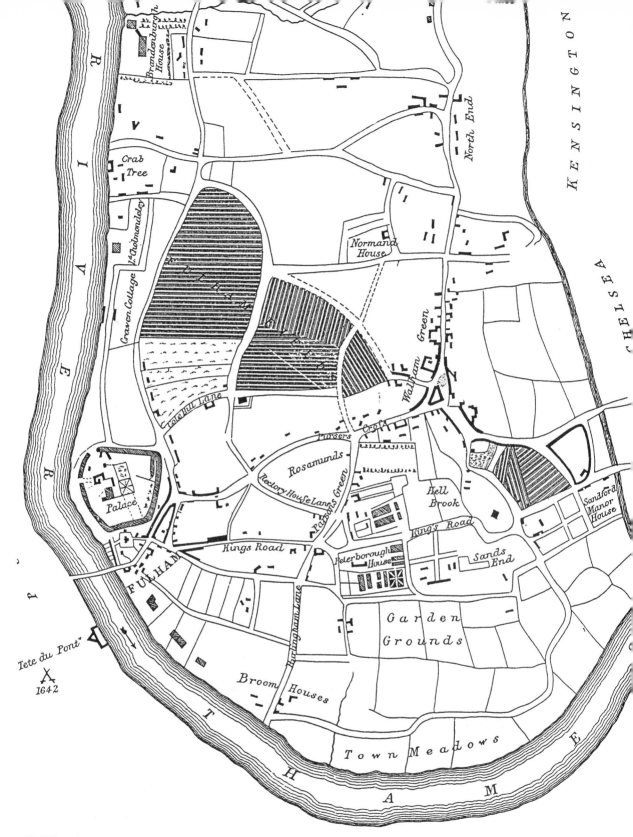

17. Fulham in 1813, published in Thomas Faulkner's An Historical and Topographical account of Fulham.

18. The King's Head, Fulham High Street, c1876.

and punishment cells – from the latter light could be excluded.

The prison closed in 1888 and was sold in 1893;[19] Burlington House itself was demolished in 1895.

In the High Street was a place called the Coalhouse, used by the parish to store coal for sale or free distribution to the poor during winter months. The parish accounts contain numerous references to the place and transactions such as that in 1640 when a bushel of coal was delivered to a woman 'shut up by the appointment of Dr. Cluett', a phrase indicating that she had been placed in isolation having contracted the plague.

On the west side of the High Street, facing the junction with Fulham Road, is the King's Head, a successor to a very old inn, which was rebuilt for the third time in 1905. The old shops on this side of the road gave way to flats, Parkview Court, in 1932.

Undoubtedly one of the finest houses in the village was Fulham Hall (sometimes called Fulham House, which was also the later name of the previously mentioned Passors). Records show residents on this site as early as 1397,[20] one of the first being Sir John de Stourton, a west-country nobleman, who served both Henry V and Henry VI in foreign wars and public offices, for which he was created Baron in 1448. The house remained in the possession of the Stourton family for over half a century but little more is known about residents until Elizabethan times when the occupants, a family called Cordell, fell foul of the Act of Uniformity and the lady of the house was fined twenty pounds for failing to attend church.[21]

The original house must have given way to a new building in the 18th century, as evidenced by an advertisement in the *London Evening Post* in 1740:

18. The King's Head, Fulham High Street, c1876.

'A compleat modern brick built house consisting of four rooms on a floor, with good stabling for eight horses and rooms over them for servants with two coach houses, a very good wash house, brew house and laundry, two very good gardens, one a pleasure garden, the other a kitchen garden, both planted and stocked with the best fruit, likewise an exceedingly fine shady elm walk, nearly a quarter of a mile in length.' The house had a large dining room with long windows opening on to the garden; the adjoining drawing room was reached through folding doors, and the library had an ornate ceiling.

William Sharp, a London surgeon at Guy's Hospital, spent the last twenty years of his life at Fulham Hall and made considerable improvements including the building of a beautiful cottage near the waterside which he named Egmont Villa, on a site acquired from the Bishop. Granville Sharp, the philanthropist, died here in 1813. He had become involved in the campaign to abolish slavery through a chance meeting with a sick negro who had been turned adrift by his master. Sharp took him into his care and when, two years later, the master attempted to regain his servant, now returned to health, Sharp resisted and the case was heard in the King's Bench; the judges ruled that a slave could not be held in this country. So strongly did Sharp feel about the issue that during the American War of Independence he gave up his post in the Ordnance Department rather than help to send arms to be used against people with whom he sympathised. He was one of the originators of the Association for the Abolition of Slavery and took a prominent part in the founding of the colony of Sierra Leone in Africa.

The distinguished Sharp family is the subject of a magnificent painting by Zoffany depicting them holding a music party on board a yacht at Fulham, an activity for which they were renowned. In the background is Fulham Church and the cottage where George II and Queen Charlotte visited them several times and took tea on the yacht, while listening to the music.

Fulham Hall was demolished in the 1840s and a number of smaller dwellings, including Cambridge House, built on its site.

Another early resident of Fulham village was Sir Arthur Aston, a Royalist in the Civil War, who commanded the King's garrison first at Reading and later at Drogheda in Ireland, where they proclaimed Charles II as King. Cromwell and Ireton took part in the attack on the rebel town and Sir Arthur, who had already lost a leg in an earlier campaign, was hacked to death and beaten with his own wooden leg.

An embarrassment to his neighbour William Laud, Bishop of London in the early 17th century, was Dr. John Everard, who was a keen opponent of the proposed marriage of Prince (later King) Charles to the Spanish Infanta. Everard had already been imprisoned in the Gatehouse at Westminster for preaching against such an alliance and had also been accused of uttering a slanderous sermon concerning the Lord Mayor and Aldermen of London at St. Martin-in-the Fields where he was a Reader in 1618. He was imprisoned several times with 'some lord or other on each occasion begging his release'.[22] These appeals led King James to ask 'Who is this Dr. Everout? He should be named Dr. Never Out!' Everard was, into the bargain, a follower of mysticism and Platonism, and in 1636 he was also charged with fatalism, anitonomianism (a belief which maintained that the law is superseded and set aside by the gospels) and with being an Anabaptist. Serious trouble occurred in 1637 when Laud, now Archbishop of Canterbury, threatened to 'bring him to a morsel of bread' because he 'could not make him stoop or bow low before him'. Everard was deprived of a living he held in Essex worth £400 a year and in July 1639 fined £1000. This did, in fact, bring him to his knees in court and, having read his submission, he was released. Everard died in Fulham in 1641 and was buried in the church for a fee of 7s. 6d. Shortly before his death he was visited by his old friend, the alchemist Elias Ashmole, whose prescription for his ills,

19. A Music Party on the Sharps' yacht at Fulham, with All Saints church in the background. Painting by Zoffany.

full of strange cabbalistic signs, can still be seen in the Bodleian Library.[23]

Also during the reign of Charles I, Fulham was home to the explorer Sir Thomas Button who, in 1612, commanded an expedition in search of a North West Passage.

A flamboyant resident was John Florio, Clerk to the Closet of Queen Anne, consort of James I. He lived in the High Street for a few years before his death in 1625, having left his house in Shoe Lane during an outbreak of plague. Florio is believed to be the person on whom Shakespeare modelled the schoolmaster and curate, Nathaniel Holofernes in *Love's Labours Lost*.[24] He taught Queen Anne Latin and French and was tutor to her son, Prince Henry. He was also author of *Florio – his first fruits – yielding familiar speech, merry proverbs, wittie sentences and golden sayings*, and seems to have had a very high opinion of himself. Shakespeare and other writers of his age probably disliked him for his sententious style of false humility, well displayed in a letter he sent to Secretary Windebank begging him to accept 'two pieces of rubbish' of which he was the author. In his will he left to the Lord Chamberlain the possibly unwelcome legacy of all his published and unpublished works, asking that the Lord should do all he could to have the dictionaries published and the profits given to his widow, Rose Florio.

A legitimate theatrical, Henry Condell, one of Shakespeare's fellow actors, had a country house in Back Lane at the same time as Florio, and for the same reason – fear of the plague. He was one of the ten principal comedians who performed in Ben Jonson's *Every Man in His Humour* in 1599 with Shakespeare, in a company known as the Lord Chamberlain's Men. This company was formally licensed in 1603 as 'The King's Servants', with Condell's name sixth on the list of members. He became a partner in the Globe Theatre, and together with Burbage and John Hemynges, who published the first collected edition of Shakespeare's plays, was remembered in the great man's will in 1615, in which he bequeathed 28s. 8d to 'my fellowes…to buy them ringes…'. Condell left his house in St Mary, Aldermary in 1625, when he retired from the stage, causing the dramatist Thomas Decker to ridicule him and other 'panic stricken fugitives from the pestilence' in a satire entitled *A Rod for Runaways*.

In 1897 Fulham's transformation from country village to urban sophistication was confirmed by the opening of the Grand Theatre, built on a triangular site now occupied by offices. Designed by the theatre architect, W.G.R. Sprague, it was ornate within and without, and surmounted by a huge statue of the Muses. The vestibule had a domed ceiling, marble columns and a staircase which led to the dress circle; the decor was in the style of Louis XIV. The first production, when it opened on 23 August 1897, was a musical called *The Geisha* and from then on the theatre was used mainly by touring companies. It closed in the early 1930s and was demolished in 1934.

20. *Fulham High Street c 1905.*

21. *The Grand Theatre. From* The Architect, *4 March 1898.*

NOTES ON SOURCES

1   John Bowack, *The Antiquities of Middlesex* (1706), Vol II, p40; Thomas Faulkner, *An Historical and Topographical account of Fulham* (1813), p266.

2   An entry in the records of the Court General in 1392: 'The Lord grants to John Hunt one garden called Godyereshauyll near the churchyard of Fulham, reserving to the Lord and his successors one way in length from the gate of the churchyard aforesaid to the footbridge beyond the great ditch [*magna fossium*] of the Lord Bishop there and the breadth xij [12] feet the which said garden called Godyereshauyll has long been in the hands of the said Lord and his predecessors as by the rolls of this Manor will appear to hold by the road as is his custom.' In the margin of the Roll against this entry occurs the word 'Goodriches' in handwriting of the time of Elizabeth I or James I. This is the house which was subsequently built in the garden and was known by that name until 1647.

3   In the Lrae. Patentes Dni. Epis. London pro officio Registrarii, there is a copy of the appointment of William Skelton as registrar to the Bishop of London, Henry Compton. (9 June, 1704).

4   Joseph Roe, *Diary*, 1807–12.

5   John J. Murray, *The Quest of the Golden Lion*, (Fulham and Hammersmith Historical Society 1981), pp37–57; Charles Feret, *Fulham Old and New* (1900), Vol. I, pp82–85.

6   Faulkner, p26.

7   *An Account of the New Manufactury of Tapestry after the manner of that of the Gobelines and of Carpets after the manner of that at Chaillot now undertaken at Fulham by Mr Peter Parisot*. Pamphlet printed in 1753 by R. Dodsley in Pall Mall, sold by Mr Cooper, Paternoster Row, copies of which are preserved at the British Museum and the Art Library of the Victoria and Albert Museum. The pamphlet was also quoted in the *Gentleman's Magazine* and other periodicals.

8   Letter from Guiseppe Baretti to his brother dated 'Plymouth 18. iv 1760'. Baretti visited Fulham's Manufactury on several occasions. Details in the *Bulletin de la Société de l'Art Français*, 3 January, 1877, p5.

9   Catalogue for auction held on 12 January 1756 at Mr Langford's House, Covent Garden.

10   Feret, Vol I, p137.

11   Vickers' will is quoted extensively in Feret, Vol I, pp89–90.

12   Feret, Vol I, pp93–98. Records of Fulham Vestry and Churchwardens' accounts.

13   Undertaking signed by J. Fitch at the order of the Vestry dated 1 May 1755.

14   Faulkner, p162

15   Workhouse Committee Book, minutes of meeting held on 2 March, 1802. 'Mr Sharp reported to the Committee the very great benefits which had resulted from the adoption of the inoculation for the cow pox and declared it was his opinion that it was by no means dangerous in itself and almost beyond the possibility of doubt effectually to prevent any person who had it from ever after having the small pox, which disorder has been lately very prevalent and destructive among the lower classes of people in this parish and its vicinity.'

16   The present Marquess of Northampton informs me that these letters were never in the archives but were sold in 1923 from the Townsend Papers. He does not know who bought them, but it was not his father.

17   Feret, Vol I, pp127–129.

18   *Prospectus* issued by Dr Laumann in 1840, illustrated with views of the school.

19   Feret, Vol I, pp127–129.

20   The London and Middlesex Fines record the sale of the messuage (the house and ground around it) in 1397 by Richard Mede to John Shirebourne, clerk. (Fines contain judgements on the ownership of land and are housed in the Public Record Office.) In Escheats 17 Edward IV, John Shirebourne and others are recorded as having sold the messuage consisting of house and garden, valued at 3s 4d per annum, in 1449 to John, the first Lord Stourton. (An escheat was the reversion to the lord or the Crown of an estate which occurred when the tenant died without heirs, where the heir had not yet attained his majority, or where the tenant had committed an offence which incurred the forfeiture of the estate.) An *Inquisition Post Mortem* Edward IV 1462 (an inquiry into the possessions of a deceased person who had held land under the Crown) records that at the time of his death 'Joh'es Stourton nde Stourton held a messuage cum gardin in Fulham'.

21   *Middlesex County Records* Vol I, p122. (For 18 March, 1581).

22   Feret, Vol I, p117.

23   Ashmole MSS 1440, fol 204.

24   William Shakespeare, *Love's Labours Lost*, Act IV Scene 2 and Act V Scenes 1 and 2. (Holfernes is believed to be a loose anagram of Joh'nes Florio).

CHAPTER TWO

The Manor Born

Research into the source of Fulham's name has been inconclusive. The English Place Names Society considered it to have been derived from the name of an Anglo Saxon chief, 'Fulla' and 'ham' (low lying land in the bend of a river).[1] Various spellings existed over the centuries – Fulanhamme, Fuleham, Foleham and Fulleham, and there was an earlier tradition that 'ful' meant foul or muddy. During recent years there has been a tremendous revival of interest in Fulham's earliest history, due almost entirely to the efforts of the Fulham Archaeological Rescue Group. This has carried out a number of interesting digs, particularly in the vicinity of Fulham Palace, which show that approximately 5,000 years ago Neolithic people were living by the riverside and in other parts of the area. Excavations have also revealed Roman settlements during the third and fourth centuries AD.

Until 1834 Fulham and Hammersmith had been a single parish, the two hamlets being known as Fulham Side and Hammersmith Side. In that year the latter became a separate parish and the curacy of St Paul's, with its chapel-of-ease, was designated a vicarage. The new boundary ran along the watercourse known as Parrs Ditch, a tributary of Stamford Brook, through Brook Green under a brick bridge at Hammersmith Road, where it was known as Black Bull Ditch. The stream then turned west under the present Talgarth Road, north of Barons Court Cemetery, went beneath Fulham Palace Road and then, via the line of Chancellors Road, to a river outlet near the present Riverside Studios. This watercourse, underground now, is part of London's drainage system. From the Parrs Ditch crossing of Hammersmith Road the Fulham boundary continued along that highway to Counters Creek, and the Thames still forms the southern and western boundaries. The northern boundary between the parishes of Fulham and Hammersmith was changed slightly in 1900, when Fèret was completing *Fulham Old and New*, to follow a devious route which excluded St Paul's School and its grounds.

The people of ancient Fulham would have used the Thames as a highway to London much more than the existing muddy lanes. The river was wider and shallower than it is today and the low lying meadows at Fulham were frequently flooded. The banks were edged with great swathes of osiers and reeds, and the surrounding countryside was thickly wooded, with the gentle slopes of the hills of present-day Roehampton and Richmond rising to the south and west. Beyond the trees, on the northern bank, the Bishop's home was no 'palace' in the modern sense, but just a country manor house surrounded by the buildings of a home farm, barns and stables. Even in the first photographs of Victorian days, before the building of the present bridge, the riverside scene was reminiscent of that which still survives at Isleworth – a church, a few houses, and an inn, the river tree-lined and reeded. The manor of Fulham was granted to Waldhere, generally regarded as the fifth Bishop of London, and his successors, around the beginning of the eighth century AD. The estate was of considerable size, being fifty hides of arable land (the hide was a rather vague unit of land measurement varying in size up to 120 acres). In the Domesday Book the Bishop's land at Fulham was valued at £40, being sufficient to support 1,000 hogs from the pannage of acorns and beech masts in its woods, valued at 17d, and his half share of the river, its fisheries and ferry fees,

22. A View taken off Wandsworth Hill looking towards Fulham. Published by Boydell in 1753.

was worth ten shillings. (The whole manor extended far beyond its present boundaries to include Ealing, Acton and Brentford, as well as other land at Finchley and Hornsey.)

As part of his obligations the Bishop maintained four bridges. One spanned a watercourse which separated 'Fulham Side' and 'Hammersmith Side' in the old united parish. The other three spanned Counters Creek – the boundary (now a railway line) between Fulham and Kensington and Chelsea. One was called Countess (later Addison) on Hammersmith Road, a second called Stamford on the Fulham Road and a third called Stanley on the King's Road. The bridge which now carries Lillie Road is comparatively modern, having been built in 1826. There was another very early crossing near Gibbs Green, which has been defunct since the early 16th century, and an obscure bridge to the south of this called Mascottes of which there are few records.

The Bishop employed a steward or reeve to collect his rents, prevent trespass and settle disputes, with beadles under him to enforce the rules. The steward would also preside over two manor courts, the Court Leete and the Court Baron. Land was rented by the system of copyhold. This allowed tenants the right to sub-lease for various periods or 'lives', thus removing most of the control from the freeholder.

The earliest forms of rents and rates in feudal England were those duties paid by tenants to the lord of the manor. They could pay pannage, for example, the right to allow their pigs to graze the woods. In 1384 just over a hundred tenants of Fulham paid pannage, from twopence for a full grown pig, to a halfpenny for a three-month-old piglet.[2] There were also restrictions on the number of pigs a tenant could own.

The estate was rich in wildlife and the lord of the manor dined well on the labours of his game-keeper. The manor also employed a mole catcher on a wage of £3 a year. The poor, harmless hedgehog had a price on its head of

23. Houses on the west side of Fulham High Street just before demolition in 1890. From a sketch by A. Beaver.

fourpence, stoats the same, weasels were valued at threepence, pole cats sixpence and sparrows threepence to sixpence a dozen.[3]

The Courts were held in the open air if the weather permitted, often on a Sunday, or in the church or the church porch, although as the centuries passed the local inn was the more hospitable venue, the King's Arms being a popular choice.

Minor misdemeanours were dealt with by the Court Leete.'Scolds', trespass of animals on the lord's land, and trading offences were dealt with by fines, although the village possessed a 'cage' for the detention of thieves and other villains, and stocks for more serious offences. The court rolls record such agricultural offences as the failure to mend fences, or to scour ditches, or the ploughing up of boundaries and the unlawful felling of timber. There were also numerous laws concerning the sale of food. Bakers who lived outside the manor were not allowed to supply bread to tenants; butchers were fined for overcharging and one for 'casting the entrails of beasts he had killed on the highway to the common nuisance'. In 1553 Stephen Claybrooke was said to keep 'two feirce dogs called mastyffs which go in the King's highway at Hammersmith to the grave danger and nuisance of people and of the king, both by day and night.' He was ordered to keep his dogs secured under penalty of 3s 4d.[4]

The manor courts also had jurisdiction over the ale houses, with strict rules as to prices and quality, two ale conners being appointed every year to taste the brews and to check the measures. The constables and beadles also toured the inns during the time of Divine Service on Sundays in order to arrest those who might be found drinking when they might be in church. Playing with dice and other forms of gambling were also dealt with by fines and some miscreants were said to 'sit up all night playing talos, sleep all day and be unwilling to work or serve when required'.[5]

24. Fulham High Street, 1895.

Rules were imposed in an attempt to give the lord of the manor some control over lodgers taken in by his tenants. It was ordered that 'such persons were of honest conversation' and in Elizabethan times anyone who gave shelter to a pregnant woman was held responsible for the child's upkeep if it were born during her stay in the parish.

Fulham's surviving Manor Court Rolls date from 1384, some of them being housed at the Public Record Office, others in the Guildhall Library. An entry in a later roll discloses that earlier records were burned during the Peasants' Revolt led by Wat Tyler and Jack Straw in 1381. The rebels hoped that the destruction of such official papers would hinder the imposition of the poll tax. Among those executed for their part in this rebellion was a Fulham boatman, John Peche.

NOTES ON SOURCES

1 Feret, Vol I, pp1–3
2 Feret, Vol I, p28.
3 Feret, Vol III, pp2 & 3.
4 Feret, Vol I, p34 (Court General Minutes 1553).
5 Feret Vol I, p29. (At a Court Leete in 1471, John Aleyn of West End (Hammersmith) was fined 12d and Thomas Fuller and John Aleyn, son of Roger Aleyn, were fined 6d.)

CHAPTER THREE

The Bishops and their Palace

'Fulham was his home and a home he dearly loved…he returned there with ever increasing delight. He might well do so, the house so spacious, yet so comfortable and domestic, the garden half hidden in the margin of the Thames, shadowed with goodly trees…' So wrote the son of Charles Blomfield, in his memoirs of his father, the great church-building Bishop of London, in the early years of the reign of Victoria.[1] No less than fifty bishops before him might well have expressed similar sentiments about their Fulham palace. His building is now secluded and almost forgotten except as a contentious issue for conservationists and politicians.

The Bishops of London had a town house, near to their 'parish church', St. Paul's Cathedral, but their summer residence was in Fulham, built on land acquired about the beginning of the 8th century when the Bishop of Hereford granted it to Waldhere, the fifth Bishop of London.[2] Hereford, it seems, made this gift 'to purge the guilt of his sins'. Not until the second quarter of the 11th century is there a record of a house on the site; prior to that the land would have been farmed and the Bishop of London, with the same obligations and privileges as any lord of a manor, found men to serve the king and received tithes and rents from his tenants.

In turbulent times some Bishops of London have been obliged to take sides and proclaim their views. Bishop Robert de Sigillo chose the wrong party when he supported Henry I's daughter, Matilda, in the struggle against Stephen; he was imprisoned and released only after a large ransom had been paid. Bishop Gilbert Foliot supported Henry II in his opposition to the views of Thomas Becket and was excommunicated by the latter. It was Foliot who had to persuade the citizens of London, after the fateful assassination of Becket, that the King was innocent of the deed and was even then keeping vigil at Becket's tomb at Canterbury. More locally, Foliot, at his death in 1186, bequeathed to his cook, William, at Fulham Palace, 'a pound of pepper per annum and the land at Fulham around the church lying between the Bishops copse and the public road to the Thames.'[3]

Involvement with state and ecclesiastical affairs quite often meant the neglect of the Fulham estate, but Richard Fitzjames, Bishop from 1506 to 1521, was responsible for many improvements to the old manor house, relics of some of which remain today. One of the earliest Bishops to be associated with the surviving structure is Thomas Kemp, who was in office from 1449 to 1488. A nephew of John Kemp, a former Bishop of London who later became Primate and took an active part in the Wars of the Roses, he is credited with having built the Great Hall c1480, which has erroneously often been ascribed to Fitzjames.[4]

Bishop John Stokesley is remembered for his presence at the burning of Tyndale's Bible at St Paul's Cross but he is also shown to have had a rather more scandalous reputation. State papers record the interrogation of the Abbess of Wherewell, a Benedictine nunnery in Hampshire, on the matter of her friendship with the Bishop of London. She was asked if she was 'familiar' with Stokesley when she was a nun, and if the Bishop was forbad entry to Wherewell and her company. She was asked, since she had a child, if she came from her nunnery to Fulham to be merry with the Bishop. She was asked if she lodged in the Bishop's own chamber for love and if the Bishop did not put on

25. Fulham Palace, 1795.

26. Bishop Edmund Bonner.

her his own kirtle 'to keep my lady warm' while she sat at supper.[5] And more besides. Stokesley was also said, while at Magdalen College, Oxford, to have christened a cat. He had also, in his first year at St Paul's, christened the later Elizabeth I.

One of Henry VIII's most promising chaplains during the long struggle to have his marriage to Catherine of Aragon annulled, was a young man named Edward Bonner. For his diplomatic services and in particular for his support of the king in dealings with the Pope, he was rewarded with the Bishopric of London in 1539. Bonner was deposed and imprisoned under Edward VI for his refusal to enforce the use of the new Prayer Book, and then reinstated under Mary. (Meanwhile, his successor to the Bishopric during the reign of Edward VI, Nicholas Ridley, a thin, passionate and ascetic Protestant, was sent to the stake.) Bonner was conspicuous thereafter for his zeal in the persecution of Protestants, which earned him a sufficient reputation to ensure his imprisonment, once more, on the accession of Elizabeth. Contemporary drawings show him as coarse-looking with voluptuous, puffy features, a broad nose, sensuous lips, clean shaven, and with short hair. Cases of heresy were often heard in Fulham church; most of those interviewed were later burned at the stake, after torture. Bonner is reported to have himself beaten one prisoner, John Miles, in the orchard of Fulham Palace with a willow rod and then 'being well nigh down to the stumps he called for a birchen rod'. He complained petulantly to the Archbishop of Canterbury of the presence of the prisoners at Fulham, 'these obstinate heretics in my house, pestering the same, are doing much hurt in many ways', and asked if they could be burnt at Hammersmith.[6]

Bonner, who died in Marshalsea Prison, was succeeded by the first of the great gardening Bishops of London, Edmund Grindal, who had spent many years in religious exile. He had the courage to be outspoken to Queen Eli-

zabeth, but is also recorded as sending her gifts of grapes from the Palace garden.[7] His horticultural interests were awakened during his enforced stay in Europe and he was responsible for introducing the tamarisk tree to England. He saw many growing in Switzerland and brought back some with him to Fulham where the soil was suitable. Grindal, responsible for the upkeep of a Fulham Palace which had been neglected by Bonner, had to meet the bill 'for divers great ruins and decays' here.

John Aylmer, a later Bishop, was criticised for playing bowls in his Fulham garden on the Sabbath and for swearing (the expression 'By my Faith!'). He remarked that Christ had said that the Sabbath was made for man, and a man might have his meat dressed for his health on that day so might he not have some convenient health for his body?[8] He became involved in a dispute about tree-felling in the area – he was accused of felling more than he needed for his own needs and selling the rest. Lord Burleigh accused him of 'allowing the wasting of his woods', and it was alleged that in four years he had sold at least a thousand timber trees.[9] Aylmer admitted some guilt but said that he had to pay the Crown taxes.

Bishop Richard Bancroft, who was one of Queen Elizabeth's chaplains, was visited several times at Fulham by the Queen during the last years of her life. On one of these occasions, in 1600, thieves broke into the Palace and stole her silver psalter. Bancroft also suffered on another occasion the theft of five of his best carpets.

27. Fulham Palace after its rebuilding by Bishop Richard Terrick in the second half of the 18th century.

28. Bishop Richard Bancroft.

One of the most interesting and certainly controversial Bishops of London, who also became Archbishop of Canterbury, was William Laud. For some years after the reign of Henry VIII, London's prelates continued to live on the edge of the political pond and even dipped their fingers in it, but in general they managed to keep out of serious trouble. Not so William Laud. He was described as 'low in stature, little in bulk, cheerful in countenance with a sharp and piercing eye, very plain in apparel and sharply checking those clergymen he saw going in rich and gaudy clothes. His learning extensive, his piety not only sincere but ardent...all his virtues partook of the warmth of his temper which entered into his religion and sometimes took him into bigotry...'[10] Although this description was doubtless by a friend its final frank words are a clue to the character which led to his execution on Tower Hill.'A public figure without a private life' is the description of Laud by Hugh Trevor Roper,[11] although he records that Laud owned a tortoise (which outlived him by a century until killed by a careless gardener) and a cat. Both creatures travelled with him from Fulham to Lambeth when he was appointed Archbishop and both escaped drowning when the wherry carrying them across the river capsized. In his first year at Lambeth was the trial of the Puritan, Prynne, a verbose and vehement preacher, opposed to Laud's view of the divine right of kings. Prynne was found guilty of a supposed libel on the Queen, imprisoned for life, fined £5000 and had his ears cut off. He had his terrible revenge, for it was he who was instrumental in securing Laud's conviction by the Commonwealth Parliament ten years later and his ultimate execution.

During the turbulent years of the Interregnum Fulham Palace was sold and the incumbent Bishop, William Juxon, despite being the prelate to escort Charles I to the scaffold, wisely kept a low profile and retired to the country. He observed that unlike others who 'flew into the King's quarters for safety' he had 'stayed at home until the Bishopric left him and roused him from his swan's nest at Fulham for a bird of another feather to build there'.[12] And very wise he was too, for he was able eventually to return to his 'swan's nest'.

The Palace and the manor of Fulham were bought from the Parliamentary government for £7,612 by Edmund Harvey, a Colonel of the Horse in the army of the Earl of Essex and a former silk-merchant. He took an active part in parish affairs, was said to be charitable and also, judging by a number of petitions, to have taken advantage of his position to rob local people.[13] Harvey gave a glittering reception for Cromwell shortly after the Protector had turned out the Rump Parliament, but his popularity with his leader was shortlived, for only a few days later he was imprisoned in the Tower on a charge of fraud in his office of Collector of Customs. A contemporary Royalist publication described Harvey as 'late a poor silk man, made a Colonel. I never heard of any that could speak of his honesty or courage, being as to the last a little inconsiderable rat...'[14] He paid a fine of £56,000 but was again in trouble at the Restoration when he was sentenced to death for his part in the execution of Charles I; he was reprieved when he was able to prove that he did *not* sign the King's death warrant.

Bishop Henry Compton lies interred in the vault beneath Fulham Church in a tomb with a fading inscription, but a more familiar memorial are the magnolia trees which open their chalice-like buds in April in parks and gardens all over Britain, a tranquil reminder of his horticultural interests. John Evelyn wrote in his *Diary* in October 1681: 'I went to Fulham to visit the Bishop of London in whose garden I saw the *Sedum Aborencens* [a variety of Stonecrop] in flower'. Compton brought back many plants, shrubs and trees from his travels and, at a time when the colonisation of America had spread the net of the Church of England, Compton was able to persuade other clergymen to send him back plants and seeds from the New World. Inventories of the Palace garden, long after his death, include Cedars of Lebanon, a Cork tree, Black

29. Bishop Henry Compton.

HENRY COMPTON.
Lord Bishop of London.

Walnut, Tulip trees, Honey Locusts, Judas Trees, Catalpas, a Virginian Red Cedar and Clustered Pine. Sadly, on Compton's death, much of his garden was dug up by his successor to grow fruit and vegetables.

30. The interior courtyard of Fulham Palace, c1798.

Compton's work, however, lived on through his gardener, George London, who went on to found one of the largest nursery gardens in London at Brompton.[15]

A Commission of Inspection, which included the illustrious names of Christopher Wren, Nicholas Hawksmoor and John Vanbrugh, was appointed in 1715 to report on the dilapidation of the Palace. It did indeed find that the building was very decayed and even if the northern parts were demolished there could still be 50 or 60 rooms left. Whatever work was done then it does not seem to have resolved the problem for, some 25 years later, in 1749, Thomas Sherlock wrote to a friend on his appointment to the Bishopric: 'I find there is a very bad old house and I must repair a great deal of it and I am afraid, rebuild some parts.'[16] Sherlock, who was Bishop for thirteen years, had a reputation for his athleticism: he was a keen swimmer into middle age and was known as the 'plunging prelate'. A story is told that when taking a dip in the Thames, and being swept by the tide to land at an orchard, he was accosted in his naked state by the owner who accused him of stealing apples. Sherlock replied indignantly that he had done no such thing, being the Bishop of London.'A likely tale' he was told.'If you are the Bishop, where is your apron?'

31. Bishop Beilby Porteus.

It was Richard Terrick, who became Bishop in the early years of the reign of George III, who demolished medieval parts of the Palace and added castellated towers and battlements to the east front which a successor, who disliked their 'Gothic nonsense', demolished.

When Beilby Porteus became Bishop of London in 1787 he was the first American to be installed on the throne of St. Paul's. An unconventional man, he shocked some of his colleagues when he came to Fulham Palace, by holding services in rooms other than the chapel. One of his favourite venues was his library, where he assembled a great collection of portraits of former bishops as well as a large number of theological books. He also built a dyke to protect the water meadows between the river and the Palace from flooding.

Bishop Charles Blomfield is renowned for his energy in building new churches in the London area. Coming to the office in 1828 he declared that his ambition was to erect fifty new churches in the capital and he donated a large sum of his own money to the cause.

A successor, Bishop Tait, lost five daughters in a scarlet fever epidemic. This tragedy, early in his married life, may well have inspired his wife to take two houses in Fulham, during the cholera outbreak of 1866, to house thirty girl orphans whose parents had died of the disease. It was Tait who built, at his own expense, a new Palace chapel, designed by William Butterfield; the old hall where services had been held then became a picture gallery.

Mandell Creighton, who became Bishop of London in 1896, loved his new Fulham home. During his brief time here he greatly improved the grounds. He and his wife were also active in measures to help the poorer people in society. Arthur Winnington Ingram, who succeeded him and held office for nearly forty years, served his clerical apprenticeship in the East End and was equally aware of social conditions. He was reluctant at first to occupy two grand furnished homes, but he realised that the grounds of the Palace could be used for local people. His housekeeping account in 1904 included the entertaining of an average of seventy working people every Saturday afternoon.

In 1884, at the suggestion of Bishop John Jackson, the Bishops Meadow, which fronted the Thames and was subject to frequent flooding, had been conveyed to the Fulham District Board of Works for conversion to a recreation ground. This was later to be enlarged to form the Bishops Park.

Just before the Second World War Geoffrey Fisher became Bishop and moved into the Palace, which he loved for its country house atmosphere despite the barrage balloons tethered in the grounds. When the bombing began he and his family slept on the ground floor in Morrison shelters, the Bishop and his wife choosing different parts of the Palace so that in case of a direct hit one of them might survive to care for their children.[17]

After the war the nature of the Bishop's work changed drastically and Fulham Palace began to be an irrelevance. In the end it was Robert Stopford who grasped the nettle of diocesan reorganisation and was, in fact, the last resident of the Palace. Henceforth the home of the Bishop was in Westminster.

In 1890 Fulham Vestry received a grant of £5000 from the London County Council towards the cost of laying out Bishops Park. The cost of erecting a river wall to prevent flooding was £12,000 alone; this was built by Joseph Mears. The wall is sunk to a depth of about 5 feet and is 9 feet wide at the base.[18] It was completed in 1893 and the park opened that year. Next year Pryors Bank was added, so that the embankment was extended to the bridge.

The old Palace garden had come into its own during the episcopacy of various 'godly gardeners', but most times it was utilitarian rather than ornamental, consisting of kitchen and herb gardens. The Palace had its own brewery, certainly until the early 19th century, with Bishop Porteus's servant praying God that the 'beer turn out good'! A tithe barn, built in the time of the Commonwealth, stored grain derived from manorial tenants; a winding path, called Monks' Walk, led to 'Bonner's chair', where that Bishop was said to have sat to try heretics. Bonner is also said to have had an orchard near the rear of the almshouses in which he had an arbour, shown variously as a rather ornate sentry box-like structure in Foxe's *Acts and Monuments* or as a dilapidated shelter between two trees in a photograph taken in 1895, and unlikely to be more than a garden store. The moat which appears in early illustrations, as an

32. Cottage by the moat of Fulham Palace.

idyllic stream that supported water lilies, later became the subject of many complaints because of its unpleasantness. Relying on the flooding tides to keep its waters sweet there were many times when it was dank and stagnant. It was filled in in 1924.

A lodge at the southern corner of Bishops Avenue and Fulham Palace Road, for the use of the Bishop's coachman, was demolished in 1872 and replaced opposite by a cottage for the park keeper. At the other end of the Avenue, turning left over the stone bridge by the Palace gates, the picturesque lodge on the east side was built in the time of Bishop Howley.[19]

The vacation of the Palace has led to much controversy as to its future and in the meantime the public has been excluded from most of its buildings. Prominent amongst those campaigning for the future of the Palace has been Keith Whitehouse of the Fulham Archaeological Rescue Group, who has made several excavations in and around it. Some of these have shown that Fulham was inhabited by neolithic people as early as 4000 BC, as well as by Romano-British settlements during the 3rd and 4th centuries AD.

In recent years conducted tours have enabled groups of people to see more of the interior beyond the Fitzjames courtyard. Mr Whitehouse believes that there are in this courtyard at least six different building phases from 1480 when Bishop John Kemp built the Great Hall. Another small courtyard, known as Chapel Court, is enclosed by the east wing, the medieval chapel being on the site of the present drawing-room and part of the lawn.

In 1987 Hammersmith and Fulham Council commissioned landscape consultants to draw up a management plan for the Palace and its grounds, at the same time gathering the views of local residents and groups. It was concluded that 'The Palace and its grounds are of local, regional, national and international importance' and that it was necessary to protect them from the vagaries of short term changes. Active steps have now been taken towards the establishment of a Museum of Fulham Palace, administered by a charitable trust on which the Bishop of Fulham will sit as a representative of the Church. An inaugural photographic exhibition in the summer of 1990 enabled many more people to visit the Palace and learn more about its history. The consultants also discovered an evergreen oak in the gardens, which they thought could be one of the oldest of the species in England, and myrtle bushes between the windows of the east front, which are said to have come from cuttings taken from Queen Victoria's wedding bouquet.

NOTES ON SOURCES

1   Alfred Blomfield, *Memoir of Charles James Blomfield, Bishop of London* (1863), Vol II, p205.
2   Feret, Vol I, p5; Leslie Hasker, *The Place which is called Fulanham* (Fulham and Hammersmith Historical Society 1981), p3.
3   Philip Whitting (ed), *History of Fulham* (Fulham History Society 1970), p165.
4   Keith Whitehouse, *A Brief History of Fulham Palace* (Fulham Archaeological Rescue Group 1982), p3.
5   *Calendar of State Papers Domestic*, 26 Henry VII, 1530.
6   RobertChambers, *Book of Days – A Miscellany of popular antiquities in connection with the calendar* (1863).
7   State Papers. Letter from Grindal to Sir William Cecil, 9 September 1569; Faulkner, p209.
8   Faulkner, pp214–215.
9   John Aubrey, *Brief Lives* (1813), Vol I, p74.
10 Thomas Fuller, *Church History* (1662), b. xi, p216; Faulkner, pp227–228.
11 Hugh Trevor-Roper, *Archbishop Laud* (1962), p35.
12 Fuller, b. xi, p216.
13 *Mercurius Politicus*, 1–8, November 1655, no. 282, p5740.
14 'Mystery of a good cause briefly unfolded', 1660. See Feret, Vol III, p186.
15 Mary Cathcart Borer, *Two Villages* (1975), p61.
16 Feret, Vol III, p107.
17 William Purcell, *Fisher of Lambeth* (1969), pp84–85.
18 Feret, Vol III, pp211–212.
19 Ibid. Vol III, p96.

CHAPTER FOUR

Down by the Riverside

Until the building of the first bridge in 1729 transportation between Fulham and Putney was by ferry. The earliest record of this is found in a document of 1210, when a charge of one penny was made for carrying the harness and wardrobe of two men and seven horses.[1] Some forty years later the harness of Queen Eleanor's horses was transported for threepence, the Queen and her ladies having crossed further downstream, possibly at Lambeth.[2] In the reign of Edward I Robert the Ferryman, of Putney, was paid four shillings for conveying the royal household to and from Fulham, using two barges and taking two days for the job.[3] Bartholomew East and John Wassingham owned the ferry in the reign of Henry V until a disagreement between them over repair of their boat; a Court Baron of 1422 records that East was ordered to build a new boat, with Wassingham paying half the cost and receiving a share of the profits.

The right to operate the ferry was a lease under the Bishops of London, this then being sublet to ferrymen. The lease was linked to certain properties, such as Passors, its ownership passing through families over the years. In 1606 it was ordered that the ferryman should pay to the lessee one farthing for each parishioner carried, one half-penny for non-parishioners and additional charges for horses. The State Domestic Papers of the Royal Household for December 1639 contain a warrant for several ferrymen at Fulham, Hampton Court and Shepperton to convey Charles I and his household across the Thames during a three-year period.

Passage across the Thames was often hazardous. In rough weather the craft was sometimes driven down as far as Wandsworth before it could reach the Surrey shore. The Fulham ferry capsized in 1633 while carrying servants of Archbishop Laud, who noted in his diary: 'I was translated to the Archbishopric of Canterbury. The Lord make me well…the day before when I first went to Lambeth my coach horses and men sunk to the bottom of the Thames in the ferry boat which was overladen, but I, praise God, lost neither man nor horse.'[4]

In November 1642, Robert Devereux, Earl of Essex, General in Cromwell's army, 'caused a bridge to be built upon barges and lighters over the Thames between Fulham and Putney' protected at both ends by earthworks.[5] Situated some distance down river from the later bridges remnants of the fort on the Putney side were discernible until 1845, when it was entirely demolished.

Ferry passengers would have embarked at Fulham on the Millbank, named from a mill mentioned in 15th and 16th century records, a stretch of shore which ran from Bishops Park to the Swan Inn some hundred yards downstream. The landing place, described grandly as a wharf, was little more than a primitive embankment. The inn, built by Christopher Gray soon after 1695, complete with brewhouse and barge house, was a three-storey building with dormer windows. Gardens ran down to the riverside so that families might spend outings there. Across the front of the house were painted the words 'good accommodation for man and beast'. A paved area in front of the house was often used as a parade ground by the Fulham Light Infantry Volunteers.

On 18 September 1871 the inn burnt down, possibly the work of an arsonist. The ironwork supporting the original sign was salvaged to surmount

33. Fulham Ferry, still in operation, c1870. The bridge is on the left and the aqueduct is on the right.

the pavilion of the Shepherds Bush Bowling Club. The site is now covered by modern flats and offices.

First attempts to bridge the river with a permanent structure met with furious opposition from the ferrymen, of course, but also from the City of London whose toll revenue at London Bridge would be affected. In Parliament, John Jones, one of the members for the City of London, stated that the water at Putney was shallow at ebb and if a bridge were built there not even the common wherries would be able to pass the river at low water. It was a wild and silly scheme...'[6] Mr Waller, another MP, was in favour. 'It seems to me,' he said, 'that if it is a bad thing for Southwark it will be a good thing for Westminster where we are...At Paris, Sir, there are several bridges, at Venice, hundreds! What then? Paris is not ruined and Venice flourishes.'[7] Sir William Thompson was concerned that a new bridge here would extend the boundaries of London away from its walls and gates and even prophesied that 'when the walls of London shall no longer be visible and Ludgate is demolished, England itself shall be as nothing.'[8] When the House divided the Bill was lost by 67 to 54 votes.

It was not until 1722 that the scheme was revived – legend has it that this was because the Prime Minister, Sir Robert Walpole, was left stranded on the Surrey bank after visiting the King at Kingston, with the ferrymen carousing on the northern side. The Prince of Wales, who used the ferry to cross to Richmond Park, added his support for a bridge.

It was at the Swan on 26 July 1726 that the Commissioners appointed to consider the matter met for the first time.[9] They eventually assessed five designs, four of which were wooden bridges, and one was merely a succession of moored boats, but none of the constructions was expected to last more than fifty years. Although the Commissioners at first settled on a design by Thomas Ripley, which had the advantage of providing a sort of scaffold on which to hang a future stone bridge if required, they revised their choice two years later in favour of Sir Joseph Acworth's timber bridge. There was also the important question of the route the bridge should take and it was decided that, leading

from the site of the horse ferry at the Swan, it would have to curve on the Putney side in front of St Mary's church to meet the approach road. The contractor was Thomas Phillips, carpenter to George II.

34. View of Fulham Bridge and Putney, c1760.

Compensation was paid to the owners of the ferry rights – the Bishop of London on the north of the river and the Duchess of Marlborough on the south, and to the ferrymen themselves. Subscriptions were then invited from the public towards the £30,000 needed to build the bridge. Subscribers included the Prime Minister himself, Sir Robert Walpole, several MPs, the Deputy Treasurer of Greenwich Hospital, Capt. Peter Solgard of Southampton, captain of the 70-gun battleship *The Berwick*, Admiral Sir Charles Wager, who lived at East End House, Parsons Green, Thomas Cranmer, described as a man-midwife and physician, William Cheselden, a surgeon at St Thomas's Hospital, and, diplomatically perhaps, the contractor himself.

Cheselden also took an interest in the design of the bridge, which seems eventually to have been a mixture of ideas from at least three contenders, with Ripley still much involved. Phillips estimated that it would cost about £10,000 and he began work on 25 March 1729.[10] In eight months the bridge was opened to traffic on 29 November.[11] Four toll men, on wages of ten shillings a week, each provided with coat, hat and staff, were engaged; tolls, on average, came to about £40 or £50 weekly rising spectacularly on special occasions, such as the review of troops on Wimbledon Common by the Prince Regent in 1811, when they went up to £100.

As part of the compensation to the Bishop of London he was exempted from tolls for himself and his household, a privilege often abused by those who had the nerve to shout the word 'Bishop' and walk or drive on!

The structure was 786 feet long and 23 feet wide with pedestrian recesses at the side. Beneath were 26 openings, the largest of which was known as

A Fulham Bridge Tollman in the Olden Times.

35. A pen drawing by A. Chasemore of a Fulham tollman imperiously asking for toll money at Fulham Bridge.

Walpole's Lock. A small toll house stood on the Putney side, and a larger one, which spanned the roadway and included the bridge manager's accommodation, at the Fulham end; each was furnished with a bell which could be rung for help in the case of disorder. In 1739 the Bridge Committee investigated a 'riot and assault by three Army officers on the persons of tollmen by beating them in a most cruel and inhuman manner.' The soldiers paid compensation of twenty guineas for this but were excused prosecution on the grounds of their youth. Conversely, the toll-gatherers themselves were in front of the King's Bench the following year charged with violent assault and abuse to the Hon. Miss Carylls, her servants and company after a dispute over the charges.

The *Gentleman's Magazine* of January 1757 notes that on 9 January one of the piers gave way from the great load of ice against it, although a coach going over at the time survived.

The bridge lasted more than the estimated fifty years, survived even a serious collision in 1870, but the passing of the Metropolis Toll Bridges Act 1877 spelt its doom. This Act transferred control of the bridge to the Metropolitan Board of Works, who freed it from toll and proposed its replacement. (Battersea and Hammersmith bridges were also to be rebuilt).

A new, stone bridge, designed by Joseph Bazalgette, was opened in 1886 on the line of an aqueduct of the Chelsea Waterworks Company, which had been built across the Thames in 1855 to bring water from the south of the river to the north.

One consequence of the new line of the bridge was that the approach road on the Fulham side no longer passed the Eight Bells, and for their loss of trade the owners received £1000 compensation. On the other hand the new road

now passed too close to the Bishop of London's premises and he had his wall raised.

Any ancient river crossing abounds with stories and legends and that of Fulham to Putney is no exception. They vary from harrowing tales of escapes from death in the swirling waters, to a romantic escape of lovers, the ferryman frantically rowing while the parents are left on the shore. Extravagance is revealed by a visitor who, arriving too early for his appointment at Fulham Palace, spent his time going backwards and forwards across the Thames to enjoy the view. There was also the cat which watched for fish under the bridge at low tide and which appeared at the toll house one night covered with mud and with an enormous eel twisted around its body.

The setting, at the time of the watermen, was idyllic. Just before the Swan, and downstream from the bridge, was Willow Bank, a late-Georgian mansion with lawns down to the river; above the bridge were Egmont Villa and Pryors Bank, the latter a mock-Gothic eccentricity which was later replaced by a mock-Tudor refreshment pavilion for Bishops Park. Nearby was Thames Bank, a two-storey, balconied house with high French windows. Upstream past the Bishop's Palace was Craven Cottage, a house now perpetuated in the name of Fulham Football Club's ground. Between here and the little settlement of Crabtree, stretches of waving osiers grew down to the river's edge in the former cherry orchards of Rowberry Mead, the basis of a local basket-making industry. Crabtree's modest Pot House became, with the increase of population, the Three Jolly Gardeners and then, as Fèret describes in 1898, 'a large and

36. Putney Bridge, as it was now called, under construction.

37. Tollgate keepers on Putney Bridge in 1880.

commodious hotel'.[12] In earlier times there were oast houses nearby, run by Joseph Attersoll, who can be considered one of Fulham's earliest industrialists. He added a chalk wharf, lime kilns and a vitriol factory to his more rural activity in the period 1783 to 1806. But these were just small intrusions when the Earl of Cholmondley decided to build Rosebank, 'the prettiest little baby house in the world', just a short distance away. Another neighbour was the mid 18th-century Dorset Villa with nearly 300 feet of river frontage, three acres of lush gardens and great shrubberies of rhododendrons. The house had a drawing room of 32 x 16 feet, a dining room leading to a span roof conservatory, a billiard room, rustic summer house, grotto, rockery, water tower, a 'dripping well', aviaries and fountains.[13] In 1832 it was taken by Guy Champion, a partner in a firm of vinegar brewers, with a strong sporting bent. He refused to attend a serious fire at the vinegar yard because his horses were ill, and his betting activities included a wager that he would ride a black horse 'right round Europe'. He did get as far as Ankara where he bid for a beautiful white slave girl in the market, brought her to England and married her.

The house was next taken by a Savile Row tailor, Henry Poole (whose firm still survives), who turned it into a popular social venue, with parties and *fêtes champêtres* for his wealthy clients, many of whom patronised him in recognition of his support for Louis Napoleon in his years of exile.

Dorset Villa was demolished in the 1870s and the site used for warehouses by corn merchants Hood and Moore and the Anglo-American Oil Company. A similar fate overtook neighbouring Belle Vue House, built in the early 19th century for John Edmonds, dentist to George IV; he was an eccentric man and was said to keep a wolf in his garden.

Other lurid stories are told about this part of the river, which was known as Cockbush. Faulkner recounts that two bodies were found when workmen were raising the embankment, one headless, one with a dagger embedded in it.[14]

No account of Fulham's waterside would be complete without mention of John Phelps, whose name is inseparable from the history of the Oxford and Cambridge Boat Race. He lived at 1 Church Row for forty years, but his family had been watermen and water bailiffs in Fulham for generations. Born in 1805 he showed early skill at rowing, was apprenticed to the river, served his time and rowed for the Doggett's Coat and Badge in 1827. It was his straightforward conduct as a judge of the Boat Race which won him the sobriquet of 'Honest John' and he retired after the memorable dead-heat in the race of 1877.

Putney might well claim more prominence in the Boat Race, for the event is usually described as being between 'Putney and Mortlake' and the boat-houses are on the south side, but many of the famous landmarks, such as Craven Steps, are on the Fulham bank. Once a highlight of the Cockney year, the Boat Race suffered a decline in general popularity in the years after the Second World War. However, in recent years the crowds are once again flocking to see the event.

Fishing rights at Fulham were owned by the manor, which leased them out, usually for a term of 21 years. Gilbert Sheldon, Bishop of London 1660–63, drew up an indenture for leasing the rights to wealthy local resident Sir Nicholas Crispe. This required him to supply 'three fair fresh salmons sweet and good' on Trinity Sunday and St John the Baptist day, as well as 400 smelts which were to be delivered between February and March to his London house.[15] Fish caught here in those days included sturgeon, lampreys, trout, flounders and eels. A cruel practice in the early 19th century, carried on by poachers, was the catching of large numbers of smaller fish, such as roach, whose scales were scraped off for use in the manufacture of artificial pearls, and the fish thrown back in the river to die.

The uncontrolled nature of the river, until the installation of the Thames

38. John Phelps, waterman.

39. The Crabtree Inn, c1895.

locks, caused frequent flooding. Phenomenally high tides are recorded in the 18th and 19th centuries, some inundating the fields of Fulham, with barges and sheep carried away and crops ruined. In February 1873 the water rose up the High Street and in March reached as far as the kitchens of Fulham Palace.[16] Although the roadway to the bridge was raised in 1875, the fear of a Thames flood has remained until the recent construction of the Thames Barrier.

In bitterly cold winters the Thames sometimes froze over, so that Frost Fairs were held. In 1789 the *Annual Register* reported that 'From Putney Bridge upwards the river is completely frozen over with people walking to and from the different villages on the face of the deep. Booths have been erected and a Fair set up with puppet shows, roundabouts and refreshment tents'. Among those who enjoyed the occasion were the Bishop of London, Beilby Porteus, and his wife.

In the 19th century the advent of steam ships introduced the concept of outings on the Thames. A poster of 1840 advertises the Second Annual Excursion in aid of the Fulham Benevolent Society on the 'commodious and elegant steam packet *The Laurel*, from Fulham Bridge to Gravesend and back, for a fare of four shillings return.[17] Outings on the Thames are still popular but what the passenger can see now on the Fulham stretch of water is much altered. Fulham lost its green riverside, mainly to industry, and this is now being superseded by commercial and residential developments such as the new Chelsea Harbour scheme. Gone are the gas works, the power station and the breweries and now the oddly named 'Saccharine factory', which had taken part of the grounds of Brandenburgh House farm in the 1870s, (part had already gone for the erection of the Haig Distillery). When the wind was in the west this factory sent its not unpleasant aroma of toasted cheese wafting over Fulham. The use of the word 'saccharine' in the title of this old-established firm is confusing, for its products had nothing to do with the sugar substitute. When the French chemist Alexandre Manbré chose the name for his company, which refined sugar and glucose,

40. One of the famous lorries belonging to Manbré & Garton.

he was thinking of the Greek derivation of sugar, the word *sakchar*. The firm moved from Booth Street in Spitalfields to Fulham in 1876.

One of the more dramatic sights of Edwardian Fulham was the powerful steam wagons used by Manbré and Garton Ltd to transport the liquid sugar and glucose. These vehicles were fueled by coke boilers, which glowed between their front axles, as they chugged through the streets with steam puffing from their squat chimneys in front of the driver's cabin. Not only did they carry the weight of the sugar but also a load of coke, which could weigh 30cwt for the journey to Birmingham. The early models had solid tyres and made a memorable din as they trundled over cobbled or wood block roads.

At the end of the First World War the company merged with that of Albert E. Berry who had founded a sugar and malt products factory in Stratford in 1906. Eight years later refiners Garton Sons and Co. of Battersea were also absorbed. It was Albert Berry who invented a new form of candy sugar for brewing and it was he also, standing on the wharfside at Hammersmith and seeing raw sugar being delivered to the J. Lyons jam factory next door, who thought of the idea of pumping liquid glucose directly to the fruit and so save manufacturing time. From this co-operation with Lyons followed in the preparation of preserves and ice creams.

In 1974 the Fulham and Hammersmith Historical Society produced a book

41. Broomhouse Dock, 1911.

on Manbré, written by Jeanne Stoddard.[18] As it happens, this celebration of the firm's centenary was also its obituary, for it was bought up then by Tate and Lyle and closed down in 1986.

Downstream from the bridge the peaceful riverside scene survived until the later years of the 19th century, with the exception of the intrusion of the gasworks in the 1820s. Hurlingham, Broomhouse and Sands End, away from the main route to London, saw few travellers. Hurlingham Road, described in early records as a 'worple', and later called the Ship or Back Lane, was no more than a footpath leading to the Town Meadows through one of the more remote areas of old Fulham – so remote that it was chosen as an area for plague burials;

a pest-house, in which people afflicted by the contagion were detained, was set up in Hurlingham Fields in 1637.[19] The parish appointed a searcher, Mary Jones, in 1647 to seek out infected people; she was paid 12d a week and her house rent, plus 6d for each search.[20]

Broomhouse, a tiny riverside hamlet, just east of Hurlingham, had only twelve rated inhabitants in 1605,[21] its main importance being that here was a dock for the ferry which conveyed passengers to The Feathers inn in Wandsworth. This appears to have been a treacherous part of the river and there are records of drownings, including one in the parish registers of 1685 telling of a 'short black man in a black waistcoat being drowned and cast ashore at the Broomhouses'.

The building of the bridge brought an end to the isolation of this part of the river and encouraged the development of substantial mansions such as Hurlingham and Ranelagh Houses, Mulgrave and Little Mulgrave, Broomhouse, Lonsdale House and others. Still surviving in Hurlingham Park is Field Cottage, now a lodge, which was rebuilt in 1856 as a solid stone building; it was used by Elizabeth Palmer, a local benefactress, in the 1860s as an orphanage and industrial home for girls, and was later sold to the Hurlingham Club for residential accommodation. Opposite is the Vineyard with its old coach house, dating from 1845, and a few doors away the Italian Villa (1809), which was once the home of James Burchell of the nursery garden family and after him, of the Victorian painter John Lawson. Back on the south side is Hurlingham Lodge, a rather grim, old grey house which fits its reputation for being haunted; it was built in 1845.

The closure of Bells Alley at the end of Hurlingham Road has saved the latter from becoming a traffic route and it still retains enough of its past charm to allow the imagination to recall the previous grandeur of the lane when it was used by the carriage trade on their way to watch polo at the Hurlingham Club.

NOTES ON SOURCES

1 E.T.D. Hardy, ed., *Rot de Lib ac de Misis et Praestitis* (1844), p155.
2 Wardrobe account, 36–7, Henry III (Carecta 1–14 Q R).
3 *The Household Establishment of Edward I* (Antiquarian Society; see Feret Vol I, p42), pp51–54.
4 Diary of William Laud, 18 September 1633, p49; Faulkner, p229.
5 Feret, Vol I, p47.
6 The Hon. Anchitelle Gray, *Debates of the House of Commons* (1769), Apr 4 1671, pp7–8.
7 Ibid.
8 Ibid.
9 Feret, Vol I, p52.
10 *Historical Register*, 31 March, 1729.
11 Feret, Vol I, p59.
12 *Ibid.*, Vol III, p85.
13 *Ibid.*, Vol III, pp82–83.
14 Faulkner, p441.
15 Feret, Vol I, p19.
16 *The Standard*, 27 February 1873.
17 Poster reproduced in *Fulham Bridge* by George and Michael Dewe (Fulham and Hammersmith Historical Society 1986) and *Life in Fulham* (Hammersmith and Fulham Libraries 1985), p31.
18 Jean Stoddard, *One hundred years of Sugar in Hammersmith* (Fulham and Hammersmith Historical Society 1974).
19 Feret, Vol III, p225–226.
20 Fulham Vestry Minutes, 18 June 1665.
21 Feret, Vol III, p249.

CHAPTER FIVE

The King's Private Road

Between the old village of Fulham and Parsons Green ran a rough track which, from the time of Charles II, was referred to as the 'King's Private Road'.[1] It was a continuation of the King's Road from Chelsea to his palace at Hampton Court via the ferry at Fulham. Subsequently much disagreement ensued as to who was responsible for this road's upkeep – parish or Crown? The Crown retained some jurisdiction over it until 1831, when its prerogative was surrendered and the road became a public responsibility, in the care of the parishes through which it passed. Until the late 19th century the section nearest to Chelsea was known as Broxholm Road and the remainder, nearest to Fulham, as Church Street.

Two old inns stood on the road. The Ship, sited near the present railway bridge, flourished in the 18th century, with tea gardens running along Hurlingham Lane. The King's Arms, one of the oldest inns in Fulham, was an alehouse in the time of Henry VIII, when the keeper was fined for failing 'to make smooth his ale pole'.[2] It is mentioned in a catalogue of *Tavernes in ten shires about London* published in 1636,[3] and in 1656 the inn-keeper, Francis Stutsbury, issued his own tokens in a period when coin of the realm was scarce. In 1686 the owner was Robert Limpany, who left an annual bequest of loaves, buns and ale to charity children, which was subsequently charged to the inn. The King's Arms was a coaching inn on the route from London to Southampton, convenient for a first change of horses; it was also used for parish meetings and dinners, one of which was held annually to commemorate the Great Fire of London. The old building was demolished in 1888 and replaced by the present structure.

On the south side of New King's Road stood Chaldon House, built *c*1750 on the site of a smaller building. Subsequent owners included two art collectors, Thomas Chinnall Porter and Charles Howell. It is recorded that the removal of Howell's furniture from his previous home at North End Grove cost no less than £287, the operation being carried out by the use of twelve cabs going backwards and forwards for a week. Howell, who moved here in 1874, restored the house and commissioned stained glass windows by Burne-Jones and Rossetti. Unfortunately the house was demolished in 1879 to make way for the Metropolitan District Railway.

Apart from its mellow golden facade in Fulham High Street, the old foundation of All Saints School is largely hidden from the public gaze by other buildings. It is difficult to be sure of the date this school originated, although it was probably about 380 years ago when Dr Thomas Edwardes, Chancellor to the Bishop of London, made a gift of £16 during his lifetime (he died in 1618) to provide a school room at Fulham Church. In 1704, a further bequest of £1,000 by Edward Owen to be used for 'pious and charitable causes' was used in part to aid the church or charity school, a gift not implemented until 1710.[4] The vicar in 1792 reported that 18 boys and 18 girls were educated in the principles of the Christian religion. All were taught to read and write and in addition the boys to 'cast accounts', and the girls to sew and knit. They were later placed in apprenticeships or domestic work.[5] When a new and more spacious school was opened in 1811 the 'Madras' system of education was adopted whereby the older pupils taught the younger ones.[6] It was one of the thousands of

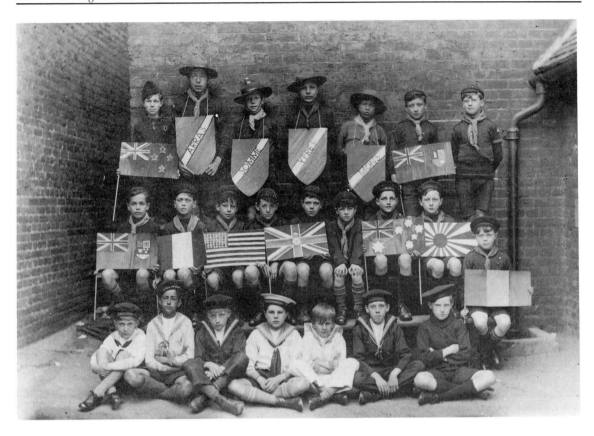

42. All Saints Primary School, c1920.

'National' schools in the country founded by the National Society for the Education of the Poor in the Principles of the Established Church. On the front wall of the Infants' School was a tablet inscribed 'Train a child in the way he should go and when he is old he will not depart from it'. The boys were given two suits of clothing, jackets and waistcoats of brown frieze (a coarse woollen cloth) with cord trousers, one for weekdays and the other for Sundays, and the girls had blue serge dresses and white straw bonnets. Despite its religious supervision the reminiscences of a visiting clergyman depict an unexpected state of affairs.'The Bishop specially commended me to the National School and I was prepared to go to them with a will. The boys' department had not quite emerged from a state of rebellion for one of the boys had thrown an inkwell bottle at the other curate's head and the school had been promptly disbanded for the holidays. When I first made my appearance I heard a hiss and I thought the next thing might be an ink bottle. I told the boy who had hissed to stand up which after much reluctance, he did. I then ordered the Pastor to flog him on the spot but taking me aside he said he dared not as the lad's father was the gardener at the vicarage. I went at once to Mr Baker [the vicar] who seemed disposed to shield the boy but I declared that unless I was supported I would quit the parish at once. The Vicar yielded, the lad was punished that afternoon and discipline was restored.'[7] The headmaster from 1826 until 1840 actually lost his reason – on his tomb in All Saints churchyard is the wording 'He was Master of the Boys National School in the parish during 14 years and was obliged to relinquish the situation by the afflictive visitation of a wise and unscrutable providence.'

43. Fulham Pottery, 1897.

A Sunday School and a School of Industry are mentioned by Daniel Lysons in his *Environs of London*,[8] which may have been linked to the charity schools, and as late as 1814 an Industry School is mentioned. A record of the work done and money earned in the Industry School survives for 1801. The seventy-six boys earned nearly £350 and the fifty girls about £382 – the girls, evidently, specialised in making underclothes, while the boys did weaving, spinning and household work.[9]

Where New King's Road bends sharply to the north east, just after its junction with Fulham High Street, one ancient kiln survives to remind modern Fulham of its famous pottery, founded by John Dwight, an Oxford man who had 'discovered the mystery of the stone or cologne wares hitherto made only in Germany'.[10] In 1671, while working as Registrar to the Bishop of Chester, he obtained a patent for making transparent earthenware 'commonly known by the names of porcelain of China or Persian ware as well as the Cologne stoneware.'[11] By 1674 Dwight was assessed for rates in Fulham as the owner of a house in 'Beare Street' and so it is reasonable to put the foundation of the pottery at just before this date. In the Victoria and Albert Museum are two pieces of Dwight pottery, one being a half-length effigy of his little daughter Lydia, whose baptism had been registered at Wigan in 1667. The child is depicted with her head raised upon a pillow, as she appeared after death, and the work is inscribed on the back 'Lydia Dwight, died 1673'. The second piece is a full-length figure of a female child with features very similar to those of Lydia. The extant Fulham burial registers do not begin until 1675 and it is uncertain if Lydia was buried at Fulham, but the absence of her name from the Wigan registers suggests that Dwight had already moved away from there. The Fulham registers do, however, record the christening of his son Edmond in 1676.

In 1678 Dwight obtained a second patent 'for several new manufactures called by the name of White Georges [a kind of pitcher], marbled porcelain vessels, statues and figures and other items never made in England or elsewhere as well as the discovered mystery of transparent porcelain and red and dark coloured porcelain.'[12] As soon as 1677 the Keeper of the Ashmolean Museum in Oxford was attesting to Dwight's innovations.

Dwight hoarded money in secret places. His notebooks record such items as '240 guineas in a wooden box in a garret hole under the fireplace', '460 guineas in the old laboratory', 'in two more holes under the fireplace 200 more guineas', and more besides.[13] His personal life was blighted by the deaths of his children – as well as Lydia, four sons died young. To make matters worse his son Samuel was disinherited for undutifulness and his remaining son entered the church rather than the business, although he did become vicar of Fulham. It is not clear what Samuel had done to incur his father's wrath. In Dwight's will, dated 1702, he is left only £5 and his mother is instructed not to give him any more until 'he shall return to his duty'. Not that Samuel was a ne'er-do-well; after an education at Westminster School and Christ Church, Oxford he entered the College of Physicians in 1731, wrote several treatises and set up a practice in Fulham.

The pottery business was carried on by Dwight's widow, joined later by her son-in-law Thomas Warland, not too prosperously it seems, for the *Gentleman's Magazine* in January 1746 reports their bankruptcy. The business was revived by another son-in-law (who married Warland's widow), William White. The Society for the Encouragement of Arts Manufactures and Commerce gave him a premium for 'inventing the art of making crucibles by British material which not only equal but excel those imported from abroad'[14] and in the following year White took out a patent for their manufacture.

Fulham Pottery was sold out of the family in 1859 after White's grandson had committed suicide in the counting-house. The business was declared insolvent again in 1888 and went to auction. The actual works remained unsold, the business goodwill and stock were withdrawn, and the remaining lots, consisting of property, were taken up. In 1891 the firm was bought by George Cheavin, a manufacturer of water filters, and his son carried on the business until his death in 1940. Much of its success during the ownership of the Cheavins came from the manufacture of stone hot-water bottles and rum jars, both of which were used extensively by troops in the 1st World War. At the height of the boom nine large bottle kilns were used, much to the dismay of neighbours who protested at the smoke; coal-firing was still used until 1957 although the release of chlorine gas had been reduced by then. One of those kilns has been preserved to mark the site of the business. After the Great War the business turned more towards art pottery and in 1929 an exhibition of its work, inspired by the MP for Fulham East, Sir Kenyon Vaughan Morgan, an enthusiastic collector, was held at Fulham Central Library – a permanent, small selection is on view there now. The exhibition also included work by other Fulham potters, William de Morgan and the Martin brothers.

The revival of arts and crafts after the 2nd World War saw the Pottery once again working in art ceramics, sometimes hand in hand with artists such as Quentin Bell, John Piper and Ivor Abrahams. In 1986, having outgrown the factory, they moved across the river to Battersea, where they now make such things as foodstuff containers for cheese, honey and mustard, in handsomely crafted red stone jars, each bearing the distinctive Fulham mark. Good collections of Fulham Pottery are held by the Victoria and Albert and the British Museums.

44. William de Morgan tile, vase design.

45. William de Morgan tile, peacock design.

46. Elysium Row, New King's Road, 1868.

Near the old Pottery, at the junction of New King's Road and Fulham Park Road, was once Elysium Row, built in 1738. Here, Mrs Tait, wife of the Bishop of London, took a house for use as a home for girls orphaned in the 1866 cholera epidemic. Among the residents of the Row were the family of Sir Arthur Sullivan and it was here that his brother, Frederick, an actor celebrated at the time as the judge in *Trial by Jury*, died in 1877, an event which is said to have inspired the writing of the famous *Lost Chord* by Arthur as he watched by his deathbed.

Just east of Elysium Row was Draycott Lodge, once the home of William Holman Hunt, the pre-Raphaelite artist; he bought it in 1879 after it had been occupied for a short while by the singer Adeline Patti. Alice Meynell, describing Hunt's home in 1893, said 'the house itself is not remarkable for its architecture. It is a house of its period and at least has the look of privacy which its period prized. It is a house which has more or less moulded itself upon the ways of its inhabitants and has been shaped by their quiet pleasures and their leisurely pursuits and necessities…the ivy has not only had time to grow but to be pruned and clipped and to grow again until it fits window and porch like a glove…' In 1899 Feret added his own description: '…the chief rooms are low and long, the drawing room and the dining room have been turned by the artist into a veritable museum of Eastern art. Attached to the house is a pleasant grassy lawn overhung with trees and cooled in Summer time by a splashing fountain.'[15]

Next door was Laurel Bank House built on the site of the old Duke of Cumberland's Head at the beginning of the 19th century. An early resident was the celebrated comedian Charles Mathews, who performed monologues called 'Mathews At Home'. Despite his popularity he was frequently hard up and his widow recalled that this was caused by the 'inconsiderate purchase of the house' owing to his 'overweening love for a country residence'.

On the south side of the 'King's Private Way', between it and Hurlingham (or Back) Road, was one of the best-known and flourishing nurseries of late 18th-century England. Fulham Nursery was established at the end of the 17th century by the Gray family, who may have been related to the innkeeper of the same name at the Swan alehouse on Fulham's Millbank. That period was important in the development of English horticulture: many new mansions were being built with extensive grounds to decorate, and travellers from abroad were bringing back plants quite new to this country. To exploit this fashion nursery gardens ringed the metropolis.

The founder's son, Christopher Gray, specialised in trees and shrubs from North America. He was a friend of the Curator of Chelsea Physic Garden, Philip Miller, and worked with him on the cataloguing and classification of American plants. He bought up the collection of shrubs and trees assembled by the Bishop of London, Henry Compton, in the gardens of Fulham Palace including, it is said, the first magnolia grandiflora in this country, from which all others were propagated. This plant lived until 1810, by which time it exceeded 4ft 10' in girth with a branch spread of 20 feet. When Faulkner described the 'Fulham Nursery and Botanic Garden' in 1813, he listed rare trees of the time including cork oaks, a Tree of Heaven (now a popular ornamental species but one which suffered badly in the October 1987 storm), the red oak and the nettle tree.[16] One of Gray's most distinguished customers was the woollen draper, Peter Collinson, who had a botanic garden at Mill Hill, on the site of today's Mill Hill School. Another customer was Horace Walpole, the writer.

47. The Baby Shop, 199 New King's Road, c1905.

48. A newsagent at 295 New King's Road, 1911.

Gray died at the age of 70 in 1764, leaving no heirs and a widow who did not involve herself in the nursery. The freehold was bought by William Burchell, a local landowner, one of whose relations, the explorer William John Burchell, opened up the area of the Zambezi and sent back plants from Africa. William John took up an appointment as a teacher and acting botanist on the island of St. Helena. In 1808 he was elected a Fellow of the Linnaean Society and made the acquaintance of a number of naturalists, including the last Dutch Governor of Cape Province, John Janssens. In 1811 Burchell travelled to the Cape to explore the interior, a venture which lasted four years, during which time he brought together a large collection of botanical specimens; in later years he travelled in Brazil. When at home he kept a small ocelot or panther in the garden of his house called Churchfield; it was here, when he was eighty, that he shot himself under a large cedar tree in front of his house, and the wound not proving fatal he staggered to a nearby outhouse where he successfully hung himself.

In 1843, when the nursery was owned by Robert Osborn, the catalogue of species for sale was described as 'being the most complete of its kind that has ever been published in this or any other country';[17] it had the added attraction of omnibuses from the Bank travelling there every quarter of an hour. When Osborn died the grounds covered 24 acres in four plots with a house, shop and warehouses on the south side of New King's Road, plus four acres opposite. The trouble was that much of the land was leasehold only, the freehold still being held by the Burchell family. In 1881, with development of the land for housing a probability, *The Gardener's Chronicle* wrote of the nursery's likely demise.'It looks like a crime to destroy...this nursery which has always been noted for the many varieties in trees seldom met with elsewhere, and its

49. Churchfield House, New King's Road, 1896.

collection of hardy azaleas.' But destroyed it was and it is still a romantic possibility that somewhere in the gardens of houses in the streets that supplanted these fertile acres remnants of the shrubs and trees survive.

The Burchell family home, Churchfield, was demolished in 1898 and the site used to build Churchfield and Ranelagh Mansions. Another house on the estate, Ivy Cottage, complete with six-stall stable and pigeon loft, had a number of interesting occupants: these included the disgraced evangelist banker Sir John Dean Paul and T.E. Smith, who promoted Mrs Bloomer, the American, whose billowing trousers set a Victorian fashion.

Near rival to Fulham Nursery was a nursery at Southfield or Broom Farm, roughly on the site of Broomhouse Road which runs from the New King's Road to the river. This business was run by the Rench family, whose prolific entries in the parish registers appear from the latter years of the 17th century. Benjamin Rench, son of the founder, cultivated the first Pine Strawberry, Chinese Strawberry and Auricula ever grown in this country, as well as experimenting with varieties of holly. *His* son, Nathaniel, added Arbutus trees and the first Moss Roses; he died, possibly at the age of 101, in 1783 and the *Sussex Advertiser* commented that it was remarkable that he had died in the same house in which he had been born and that he had had thirty children by two wives. An obituary in the *Mirror* said that the elm trees planted in Birdcage Walk were from saplings reared in Rench's nursery.

In its last forty years the nursery was acquired, like a number of others in

London, by the Veitch family of Chelsea, whose business was described as 'gigantic and one of the most prominent in England perhaps in Europe'. Fulham Council acquired the site in 1901 and also the adjoining estate of the Sulivan family, and here opened the rather prim municipalised open space called South Park in 1904. The opening ceremony was enlivened by the gates sticking, which prevented the crowds from entering, and by the mayor performing his duty without his chain of office because the key of the Town Hall strong room, in which it was kept, had been mislaid.[18]

The Sulivan family, which bought Broom House in 1823, were local benefactors. Laurence Sulivan, grandson of the first owner, distressed by the condition of the poor and the lack of education for their children, endowed a free Ragged School in Broomhouse Lane, called the Elizabethan School in memory of his wife Elizabeth. This ornate, Tudor-Gothic building was acquired by the London County Council in 1904 and became a school for tubercular children in 1921; it was later a youth club.

One of the few remaining old houses in this part of Fulham, Broom Villa, is on the east side of Broomhouse Road. This residence was probably well over a hundred years old when William Bell, owner of the Crown Brewery in nearby Peterborough Road, bought it in 1818. Fèret was able to describe Peterborough Road as having 'few buildings other than the prim red brick villas which lined its eastern side' from New King's Road to Broom Farm. Opposite were 'four or five flat fronted houses', one of which bore a plate inscribed 'Peterborough Place 1792'.[19] After the Crown Brewery on the corner of Bells Alley, the way to Town Mead 'degenerated to the dimensions of a rural path'. That path now contains numerous shops and small factories, a secondary school and various commercial buildings before it reaches the dockside Carnwath Road.

The then exclusive Peterborough Estate was built in the 1890s, principally by Jimmy Nichols, with expensive houses each decorated with his symbol of a seated lion – to the delight of modern estate agents who describe them as 'much sought-after Lion Houses'. More recent developers have created new private estates such as Hurlingham Square, entered through electronic gates, 'designed in classical architectural style', but with 1980s features such as whirlpool baths, antique bathroom brass and mahogany toilet seats, of which Jimmy Nichols would surely approve.

NOTES ON SOURCES

1   Feret, Vol II, pp62–63; Gillian Bebbington, *London Street Names* (1972), p190.
2   Feret, Vol II, p58.
3   John Taylor, *Catalogue of Tavernes in ten shires about London* (1636).
4   Feret, Vol I, p168.
5   'LCP' leaflet produced for All Saints School, 1986; Feret, Vol II, p43.
6   Faulkner, p163.
7   R. Haddon (compiler), *Reminiscences of Prebendary Rogers, Rector of St Botolph's, Bishopsgate* (1887), Vol III, p220.
8   Daniel Lysons, *Environs of the City of London* (1796), Vol II, p258.
9   Feret, Vol II, pp42–43.
10 Patent granted to John Dwight in 1671, no 164; Feret, Vol II, p47.
11 *Ibid*.
12 Patent granted to John Dwight, June 1684, no 234.
13 Feret, Vol II, pp50–51.
14 *Ibid*., pp54–55.
15 Archdeacon Farrar and Alice Meynell, *Art Annual* (1893), 'Life and Work of Holman Hunt', pp25–30.
16 Faulkner, pp19–20; Feret, Vol II, p71.
17 E.J. Willson, *West London Nursery Gardens* (Fulham and Hammersmith Historical Society 1982).
18 *Fulham As It Was* (1983).
19 Feret, Vol II, p131.

CHAPTER SIX
Green and Pleasant Lands

Parsons Green, long considered the most aristocratic part of Fulham, was described by Bowack as 'inhabited mostly by gentry and persons of quality'.[1] Mention of the timber rights attached to the Green occurs in the Court Rolls as early as 1391; in 1456 the same records note that Agnes Hesele had cut down two elms without licence. In 1625 there were only six rated inhabitants for the area.[2]

The Green derived its name from its ownership by the local rector, whose house stood nearby. Bowack recalls that in front of the rectory was 'a large common which within the memory of ancient inhabitants now living was used for a bowling green for the Rector and his domestics'.[3] In 1834 a cricket match took place between two teams of women, one of single and the other of married women, which the latter won.[4] Towards the end of the south-east corner of the Green was a pond used by horses, dogs and ducks and also by local baptists for total immersion of converts. The pond, fed by a natural spring, dried up when main drainage was laid in the New King's Road, and was then filled in.

On three days in August the annual fair was held on Parsons Green. It was a mixture of stalls, booths, puppet shows, competitions and entertainments. John Phelp, whose mother sold oysters there, recalled that 'The canvas booths were ranged about the trees, selling gingerbread and such like. It was a wonderful nice fair, apart from one thing that was not nice, poor live cocks used to be tied up by their legs and people threw sticks at them...'[5]

Few of the handsome houses at the edge of the Green now remain. Holly Bush House, later known as East End, survived until 1884; originally built in Elizabethan times, its first known occupant was Sir William Billesbie. In the mid–17th century it was acquired by Robert Blanchard, a goldsmith and partner in the distinguished private bank of Child and Company in Fleet Street. The bank was actually established by the Wheeler family and both Blanchard and Francis Child entered the firm by marriage. On the death of Blanchard's widow, Child, who had fifteen children, inherited this house which, in 1720, was tenanted by Admiral Sir Charles Wager, knighted for his part in the wars of the Spanish Succession in 1708. Wager was in command when four English ships attacked a Spanish fleet of 17 galleons, and sank the flag-ship, which carried an estimated £7 million in gold and silver. The Admiral managed to save about £100,000 in prize money for himself.

In 1808 the house's most celebrated tenant arrived – Mrs Fitzherbert, mistress, and later the wife of the Prince of Wales. Their marriage, kept secret but still widely known, would not have been recognised by either the King or Parliament if it had come to the crunch, since the widow Mrs Fitzherbert was a devout Catholic at a time when the majority of the House of Commons had no intention of removing the civil disadvantages of Roman Catholics, let alone have one as a Queen. The matter was resolved to an extent when the Regent convinced himself that he had not been truly married to Mrs Fitzherbert in the first place and this allowed him to marry the ill-chosen Princess Caroline of Brunswick, by whom he hoped to settle the succession and his own debts.

At some stage Mrs Fitzherbert's house was rebuilt in Queen Anne style and its interior fitted with oak panels and shuttering. There were 16 acres of grounds, planted with a rose garden, orangery, orchard and fruit gardens, as

51. The staircase at East End House, Parsons Green, pre 1884.

52. Maria Fitzherbert, by Sir Joshua Reynolds, c1788.

53. Parsons Green, 1890. Oil by Miss C. Sulivan.

well as with many fine trees and lawns, including a cedar which, when the land was being cleared for building, was so substantial that it had to be blown up with gunpowder.

Elm House, which still stands fronting the Green, was said to have sheltered Sir Francis Bacon after his banishment from the court of James I. By 1729 it was described as a 'large convenient house with orchard and gardens, well planted, stables, coach house and outhouses with a row of large elms planted before the gates pleasantly situated on very healthy ground. The house is fit for either courtier, merchant or large boarding school',[6] and, indeed, the latter was to be its fate, for in 1803 the Rev William Pearson began a boys' school here. In 1890 it was a Roman Catholic School of Discipline for Girls, or reformatory. This must cause wry smiles among the pupils of Lady Margaret School, one of Fulham's most progressive and prestigious educational institutions, which acquired the house in 1937 to add to its neighbour, Belfield, owned by them since 1917.

Belfield shares with East End an association with the rakish sons of George III, since the Duke of Clarence, (later William IV), kept his Mrs Jordan here. Her former name was Dorothy Bland and she made her acting debut in Dublin when she was fifteen, coming to England in 1782. Three years later she took the part of Peggy in *The Country Girl* and soon became a society favourite. It was about this time that the Duke fell in love and began to live with her; they had ten children of whom eight survived. The alliance broke up on the King's

54. *Parsons Green, c1904.*

insistence that his various sons set themselves seriously to the business of legitimate marriages and so produce an heir to the line.

Marks of Mrs Jordan's residence at Belfield included a carved fireplace bearing the monogram W and J, for William and Jordan. A later resident was the Victorian painter, Theodore Roussell, who bought the house in 1890; he opened up those windows which had been blocked off to avoid payment of window tax, and the handsome staircase was stripped of years of paint to reveal its original beauty.

The use of the house as a school began with Miss Enid Moberly Bell, daughter of the famous *Times* foreign correspondent and manager. Miss Bell was a teacher at the Whitelands Training College in Chelsea when it was decided to close its demonstration school for teaching practice. She led an influential campaign to revive it and finally a new school was opened under her charge at Belfield, a property which was purchased for £2,250. Conversion of the building necessitated the removal of some 'angled fireplaces' (including that with the monogram of William and Mrs Jordan) and although initially offered to the Victoria and Albert Museum in 1917 they eventually, together with some doors, found their way into the possession of a Mr Harper of no. 2 Swan Walk, Chelsea who, it seems, sold them on.

The school was opened by Princess Marie Louise in December 1917, its new name being Lady Margaret School in honour of Lady Margaret Tudor, mother of Henry VII, the founder of St John's and Christ Colleges, Cambridge. It has since expanded, not only taking over Elm House but also Henniker House next door. Although transformed internally the facades of Belfield and Elm House have been maintained.

Henniker, no. 9 Parsons Green, marks the site of three successive houses, the most ancient of which was known as 'Stoutes tenement' in the manorial records of 1391.[7] It was replaced during the reign of William III by a handsome

55. Rosamunds, Parsons Green, 1896.

mansion called Albion House which came to be used as a school, one of whose pupils was the young Robert Banks Jenkinson, later the Prime Minister, the Earl of Liverpool. This school was short-lived. The house was demolished in 1830 and another residence, Park House, erected in 1841 by Thomas Cubitt, 'designed to last 1,000 years'. In the late 19th century this was taken by the Fulham Board of Guardians to house pauper children. Cubitt's building did not last very long, however – it was demolished in 1889 and Henniker House, named from Jane Livesey Henniker, the first woman member of the Fulham Board of Guardians, replaced it.

Five of the terraced houses on the east side of Parsons Green near the White Horse, nos. 3–7, were bought in the 1870s by the philanthropic Frank Holt Yates, who offered them, rent free, to the London Female Preventitive Reformatory Institution for 'friendless, respectable girls'. An old photograph of the inmates, who were trained in domestic service, shows them at a long table in the garden having tea, dressed in their stiff, starched uniform dresses with bibbed aprons and little pointed caps, with streamers at the back. The site of the buildings was taken by the Council for a new Maternity and Child Welfare Centre in 1937.

The White Horse pub, at the north-west corner of Parsons Green, was rebuilt in the 19th century. It is mentioned in the parish records in 1777 and it had a unique right to a square foot of ground on which to erect its sign. The White Horse was the headquarters of Fulham's pioneer cricket club, Albion.

Near where the railway bridge crosses Parsons Green Lane were some old houses which included Blenheim House, once occupied briefly by Count Felice Orsini, one of the leaders of the French Revolution. He sought refuge in England in 1856 after escaping from prison in Mantua, but two years later was executed for attempting to assassinate Napoleon III. Nearby was a house, grown from a cottage to a ten-roomed dwelling, named Rosamund's Bower by an occupant, the writer T. Crofton Croker, in the 1850s. Croker, born in Ireland

of a military family, devoted much of his early life to collecting legends and songs from Ireland. In the 1850s he produced his *Walk from London to Fulham*, first serialised in *Fraser's Magazine* and published in book form in 1860. Blenheim House and its surrounding houses were all demolished by the Metropolitan District Railway in 1892.

56. Samuel Richardson's house at Parsons Green.

Sir John Powell of the Pay Office, Whitehall, built a large house, first known as High Elms and later as Park House, on the north-west corner of Parsons Green Lane at the junction with Fulham Road. This building was also known as Purser's Cross, an allusion to a highwayman of that name who had shot himself on capture at this spot in 1738. Yet another boys' school was established in this building; this had the future Lord Bulwer Lytton as a pupil: he was later to settle in a house by the Fulham riverside.

Rectory Road marked the boundary between the former free lands of Rosamunds and the glebe lands of the parsonage – those owned by the rector and upon which manor tenants had to work for specified days of the year. Until early Victorian days it was called Muddy Lane, its only habitation a wooden hut. It is now called St. Dionis Road to complement the church which occupies its eastern end. The Rectory itself, rebuilt in 1707 on the site of previous parsonages, was a simple square brick building with a red-tiled roof and rows of small dormer windows. Early holders of the estate included a Dr. Drewell who was reprimanded in the mid–15th century for lopping elm trees without permission,[8] Sir William Butts, a physician to Henry VIII, the widow of Sir Francis Walsingham, and Edward Limpany who was fined £5 in 1680 for failing to provide a bull and boar to service his tenants' cows and sows.[9]

For the last fifty years of its life the rectory was used for various schools, including a Military Academy; in 1882 it was demolished for the erection of St.

57. Samuel Richardson.

Dionis church and its vicarage. The building of this church was funded from the sale of the site of St. Dionis Backchurch in the City of London, a Wren building demolished in 1878 as being redundant; the oak pulpit, possibly designed by Grinling Gibbons, marble font and altar table were brought to Fulham.

Samuel Richardson, the novelist, lived in a picturesque house facing Parsons Green from 1754. It is sometimes suggested that his house was that used by Catherine of Aragon, who was then the widow of Arthur, Prince of Wales and sister-in-law to Henry VIII, whom she later married. A letter from her father-in-law, Henry VII, tells her that the house at Fulham had been kept for the ambassadors of the King of Castile, but if she wished to go to it and thought her health would be improved by being near to him, he would certainly put it at her disposal and the ambassadors would have to go elsewhere.[10] Richardson moved here from the Grange at North End, possibly to be nearer Fulham Church where he was a devoted worshipper. His villa and its grounds were swept away in 1811 and supplanted by Aragon House, Gosford Lodge, and Pitts Place. This terrace still remains on the south side of the Green. The first house became the Duke's Head public house in 1893, but the others still retain their original names, Albyn, Cardley, Sefton and Belgrave, and the date 1795. An eccentric 19th-century resident was Dr James Keats, who visited his patients wearing a long, shabby, dark-green coat with brass buttons, popularly known as 'Dr. Keats's Livery'; despite his shabbiness he could afford to keep a pack of harriers which he ran at Wimbledon Common.

Charles Fèret, writing in 1896, records that Peterborough House was about to be demolished.[11] This mansion's predecessor, part of an estate referred to in early manorial records as Brightwells, had, by the 16th century, provided a home for various members of Court. It is thought that the house was rebuilt by Thomas Carey, second son of the Duke of Monmouth, in the reign of Charles I. He employed the painter Francis Kleine to create heroic murals and ceiling paintings. Carey's widow married Solicitor General Edward Herbert, whose name, in a 1653 list of exiled Royalists, is given as living at Parsons Green.[12] The sons by that marriage each achieved distinction after the Restoration. One became Admiral of the Fleet, another Solicitor General (who went with James II into exile), and the other joined the army. The house itself was inherited by a daughter of their mother's first marriage to Carey, who herself married Lord Mordaunt, the son of the 1st Earl of Peterborough. Mordaunt, a Royalist, was imprisoned in the Tower in 1658 as part of an alleged plot but, with much good fortune, escaped conviction.

Lady Mordaunt's diary, which she kept for over twenty years from 1658, contains many interesting references to the Restoration, the Plague and the Great Fire.[13] No sooner was Mordaunt at liberty than he courageously set to work to accomplish the restoration of the monarchy; his efforts were rewarded when he accompanied Sir John Grenville to the Continent, after the death of Cromwell, to see the exiled King and to return with the Declaration of Breda which paved the way for the King's return. Mordaunt, of course, was showered with honours by Charles II. He lived much of the last fifteen years of his life at Parsons Green, gardening being one of his main recreations. John Evelyn visited him here and he records in his *Diary* that Mordaunt taught him how to make a hot bed, and was much impressed by his horticultural talent.[14] That other diarist, Pepys, was not so taken with Mordaunt's talent for writing poetry and described his verses portraying sea battle adventures as 'sorry things'.[15] Pepys also dwelt on a 'disgraceful incident' between Mordaunt and the daughter of the Surveyor of Windsor Castle which Feret prefers not to amplify.[16]

Mordaunt died at the age of 49 in 1675. Evelyn notes that in December that

58. *Peterborough House, c1800.*

year he visited his widow when 'The pious woman delivered to me £100 to bestow as I thought fit for the release of poor prisoners or charitable uses.' Her eldest son, Charles, the 3rd Earl of Peterborough, had a distinguished military career and was one of those instrumental in placing William of Orange on the throne, but he seems to have been a petulant, childish and vainglorious character.

Thomas Bowack, a contemporary of Charles Mordaunt, described the Fulham house of the time: 'The seat is very large, a square regular pile of brick and has a great gallery all around it upon the roof. It has an abundance of extraordinary great rooms with fine paintings etc but is mostly remarkable for its spacious gardens, there being about twenty acres of ground.'[17] In the house Mordaunt entertained many of the *literati* of the day, including Addison, Swift and Pope. Several of Swift's letters mention the Earl's hospitality and one of his verses begins 'Mordaunt fills the trump of fame, the Christian world his deeds proclaim and prints are crowded with his name'.[18] His activity of body and mind, said Swift, was 'incessantly hurrying him into suspicious designs and perils of a thousand kinds',[19] and Peterborough certainly loved to journey around Europe as far as the limited transport of the day allowed; it was said that he had 'seen more kings, princes and postillions than any other living man'.[20] Voltaire visited him in 1727 and stayed at Parsons Green for three weeks.[21]

Peterborough's first wife, whom he had married young and who bore him five children, died in 1709 and in his old age he secretly married a singer called Anastasia Robinson who, even after the marriage, was kept in another establishment. She was officially recognised as the Countess and allowed to wear his wedding-ring only when it was necessary for him to have a hazardous operation to remove a kidney stone. He died on a convalescent trip to Lisbon in 1735.

At the end of the 18th century the house was tenanted by John Meyrick, one of the founders of the Fulham Volunteer Corps. Meyrick, who lived previously at Westfield House in Fulham Road, (this later became the first public library in the borough), did not find Peterborough House to his taste and decided to rebuild it. His new house, at the same distance from the road but considerably to the east, was a low, Georgian building, two storeys high in the main section, with many of the main rooms in French style with rounded corners.

Later residents of this house included the immensely rich William Beckford the younger, author of the romantic novel *Vathek*. In 1845, when the house was up for sale, it was described as 'a mansion in every way calculated for a family of distinction'.[22] The front door was approached by a fine semi-circular flight of double steps with Corinthian columns on either side and the vestibule featured a circular stone staircase. The drawing room was 45 feet long extending from the front to the back of the house, and the walls were covered with moiré silk. At the rear of the house there was a pretty circular boudoir with blue walls and a painted ceiling with French windows opening on to the sloping lawns. The extensive grounds, some of which were let out as market gardens, included many types of trees.

In the Court Rolls of 1386 appears the place name Astons or Austins Field, which applied to an extensive tract bordering on New King's Road between Parsons Green and Eelbrook Common. It was let out in strip form by the lord of the manor and there is a multitude of references to its maintenance and care in the records. Eelbrook Common, a dangerous swamp, was part of the manorial waste land, at that time about 13 acres in extent. The spelling of the name is 19th century, Hillebrook or variants of that, being the more ancient name. By the 18th century the common was in a deplorable condition, being described as 'overflowing and little use or benefit for want of cleansing and scouring the ditches, for reason of certain floodgates and whelms [bridges], erected for the draining thereof being much out of repair and in decay. The water continuing upon the said commons makes the same noisome.'[23] Tenants using the common for grazing their cattle were obliged to contribute towards a draining programme. But still in 1727 it was reported that 'Hellbrook' was a wet piece of common and the overseer would probably need help to scour and clean the ditches and lay material over the 'boggy sloughs'.[24] In 1878 the Ecclesiastical Commissioners enclosed the portion of the common fronting Crondace Road with a view to selling it. This inspired a protest meeting held at Beaufort House from which a number of the more militant marched and burned the fences around the common.[25] The Commissioners abandoned their plans. Charles Feret commented in 1901 that until comparatively recent times a twelve-foot ditch ran around the common with another across the centre, these being well stocked with carp, tench, roach and eels, and that an otter had been caught there in the 1830s.[26]

In 1892 the old Peterborough Arms was replaced by a new Victorian pub, the Peterborough Hotel (now the Southern Cross), near the corner of Wandsworth Bridge Road. This road was cut through the fields and market gardens

59. *Aeroplane over Eelbrook Common, 1916. By R. Randall.*

to the bridge, providing a new route into London: it helped to change the sleepy suburb of Fulham into a development area.

NOTES ON SOURCES

1   Bowack, Vol II, p37.
2   Minutes of Fulham Court General, 1456.
3   Bowack, Vol II, p58 (supplement).
4   Feret, Vol II, p88.
5   *Ibid.*, Vol II, p89.
6   *Country Journal*, no. 157, 5 July, 1729.
7   Feret, Vol II, pp104–107.
8   Minutes of Fulham Court Baron, 1457.
9   Minutes of Fulham Court General, 1680.
10 State Papers, 28 October 1506.
11 Feret, Vol II, p156.
12 *Ibid.*, p137.
13 *The Private Diary of Elizabeth Viscountess Mordaunt Duncairn* (1856). Original MS discovered nearly 200 years later at Dundalk House, seat of the Earl of Roden, who published it.
14 John Evelyn, *Diary*, 2 December 1675.
15 Samuel Pepys, *Diary*, 22 December 1664.
16 Feret, Vol II, p142.
17 Bowack, Vol II, p45.
18 Feret, Vol II, p146.
19 *Ibid.*
20 *Ibid.*
21 *Ibid.*
22 *Ibid.*, p154.
23 Presentment to Fulham Court Baron, 1727.
24 Feret, Vol II, p78.
25 *Ibid.*
26 *Ibid.*, p79.

CHAPTER SEVEN

The Rival Village

It was the tradesmen and fretful businessmen who persuaded London Transport to change the underground station name from Walham Green to Fulham Broadway. From this time the older name began to disappear from currency and it is now virtually unknown, even to residents.

The old hamlet was described by John Bowack in the early 18th century as housing mainly gardeners, one of whom, Bartholomew Rocque, a Huguenot, eulogised Walham Green in a poem in *The London Magazine* in 1749. (His more famous brother was the cartographer, John Rocque, whose maps of London and the surrounding area, including Fulham in 1741 and 1745, are the basis of much historical knowledge.) Walham Green originally had its own manor house and village pond – the latter, long a receptacle for rubbish and dead animals, was filled in by vestry labour in 1814. The triangular green was railed around in 1721; later, Broadway Buildings (now replaced by a modern office block) were built on its site between the Broadway and Vanston Place. At the north-west corner of the green were stocks and whipping post, last used in 1826 when two men were punished for stealing fruit. Opposite, on the site of the electricity showrooms, was the parish pound in which stray animals were kept. This is mentioned as early as 1442 when a horse, ox and boar were there, and only released to their owners on payment of fines.

Fulham's first police station was built in Lewis's Yard behind the George Inn in Fulham Road in 1830. Law and order since the the 16th century had been the responsibility of unpaid constables and headboroughs, whose other duties included the apprehending of vagrants and the apprenticing of orphans. The accounts of the churchwardens in 1583 include the purchase of a corselet with pike, sword and dagger, two hargobushes (blunderbusses) and two morryons (helmets).[1] This system of unpaid, and quite often unwilling, officers was unable to cope with the increased crime of later times and the residents of Fulham in 1802 followed the same course as a number of other places in London in forming what was, in effect, a vigilante group, or 'Association Against Robberies and other Depredations committed within the Parish'; this was a short-lived venture and was replaced in 1818 with another scheme for which ratepayers subscribed on an individual basis for protection.

The situation, of course, was far worse in the metropolis and only by 1829 did Sir Robert Peel persuade Parliament of the need for a Metropolitan Police Force. The new organisation's authority did not extend to Fulham and, indeed, it was resented by many of the vestries which *were* included. Fulham Vestry decided to pre-empt any extension to Fulham by establishing a parochial police force under its own control, but this encountered legal difficulties and eventually the parish was policed by the Peelers.

Fulham's first fire station was built on the south side of Fulham Road opposite the Wheatsheaf, in 1869, four years after the establishment of the Metropolitan Fire Brigade. Previously fire-fighting had been undertaken by the brigade of the fire insurance companies; insured properties carried a metal firemark – one of these, that of the Hand-in-Hand Insurance Company, may be seen on the front of one of the old houses in Church Gate. This first fire station was rebuilt in a larger form in 1895, this time containing living quarters and stables for the horses.

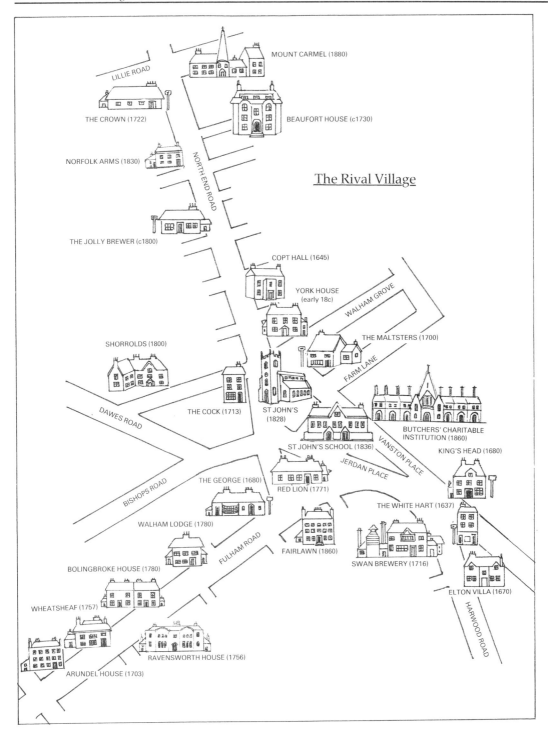

MOUNT CARMEL (1880)

LILLIE ROAD

THE CROWN (1722)

BEAUFORT HOUSE (c1730)

NORFOLK ARMS (1830)

NORTH END ROAD

The Rival Village

THE JOLLY BREWER (c1800)

COPT HALL (1645)

YORK HOUSE
(early 18c)

WALHAM GROVE

SHORROLDS (1800)

THE MALTSTERS (1700)

FARM LANE

DAWES ROAD

THE COCK (1713)

ST JOHN'S
(1828)

BUTCHERS' CHARITABLE
INSTITUTION (1860)

ST JOHN'S SCHOOL (1836)

VANSTON PLACE

KING'S HEAD (1680)

JERDAN PLACE

BISHOPS ROAD

THE GEORGE (1680)

RED LION (1771)

THE WHITE HART (1637)

WALHAM LODGE (1780)

FULHAM ROAD

FAIRLAWN (1860)

SWAN BREWERY (1716)

BOLINGBROKE HOUSE (1780)

WHEATSHEAF (1757)

ELTON VILLA (1670)

HARWOOD ROAD

RAVENSWORTH HOUSE (1756)

ARUNDEL HOUSE (1703)

60. *A sketch map of the Walham Green (Fulham Broadway) area showing many of the buildings mentioned.*

61. *Walham Green Station, c1911.*

62. *Fire Station in Fulham Road, c1906.*

63. The new Swan Brewery at Walham Green. From the Building News, *24 March, 1882.*

Fulham Court, built in 1931 by the borough on the south side of Fulham Road, is on the site of Ravensworth House,[2] a mansion built in 1756 for John Ord, Master in Chancery, who was another local and famed horticulturalist; his claim to have introduced the moss rose into the country is contested by Rench's nursery of Sands End. A contemporary writer, Priscilla Wakefield, in her *Perambulation of London* describes Ord's garden as a 'fine show of trees and plants from foreign climates but nothing so striking as a bed of moss roses measuring nearly 150 feet in circumference spread from a single stem in the centre, and spread over the ground like a carpet of the most exquisite beauty'. Ord's brother-in-law, Lord Ravensworth, inherited the house and made it, in the reign of William IV, famous for its entertainments and its guests, who included royalty: a triumphal arch was erected across the Fulham Road in 1840 for the visit of Queen Victoria.

By 1880 this house, once the resort of 'feathered songsters including the nightingale' was a hospital for women, and then the grounds were covered with the Swan brewery. The house itself, with a frontage of nearly 200 feet, had 18 bedrooms, which was just as well, since Ravensworth had sixteen children.

Swan Brewery was founded in Walham Green in 1769 by Oliver Stocken, on a site which included the remains of the old Manor House[3] – Wendon House or Dowbellers, and marked now by the White Swan public house. The busi-

ness flourished and his small beer was considered 'better than any fourpenny ale to be obtained in Fulham'. The brewery, by then on its later site in the grounds of Ravensworth House, closed in 1929.

Between the second brewery site and Walham Green, on the south side of Fulham Road, notable houses included Fairlawn, acquired by the YMCA in 1891, Berwick House (now covered by King Edward Mansions), used by the Vestry from 1866 until the Town Hall was built, and opposite the George pub whose landlord in the 1860s, Richard Hartley, combined his job with another in the Bank of England and also the running of an omnibus company.

From the George to Dawes Road there have been three major developments in the last eighty years. On this stretch of road was once the shop of John Knights, the most important butcher in the area, who was known as 'King of Walham Green'. The terrace in which it stood was demolished to make way for Mason's OK Sauce factory, a large employer of female labour before the 1st World War. This in turn was supplanted in the 1930s by the Regal Cinema and it has now been redeveloped as a supermarket.

The church of St. John was built on the site of the old village pond in response to a need for a place of worship for the growing population of this new Fulham centre.[4] Designed by J.H. Taylor (with extensive alterations in the 1890s), it was consecrated in August 1828. A few years ago the outside was cleaned but inside the problems of many 19th-century churches remained, such as crumbling plaster and an unpredictable heating system of outmoded design. Money from the sale of the redundant parish hall has now been used to convert the interior to a two-storey building, providing areas for worship and for a community counselling service. These changes have not affected the old

64. Workers in the OK Sauce Factory, c1920.

65. St John's, Walham Green, c1828.

66. The Granville Theatre, Walham Green, c1900.

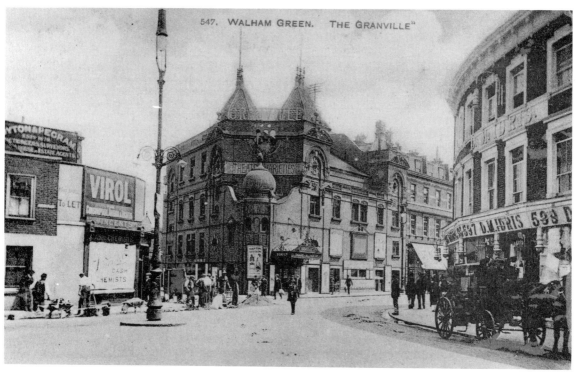

churchyard, in which over 500 people lie buried (closed in 1853), or the ancient mulberry tree which leans over them. St John's is Fulham's second oldest church school, first built on the green in 1836 at a cost of £797 for 111 boys, 73 girls and 76 infants. When it outgrew that home it moved in 1894 to its present site at the rear of Mitford Buildings in Dawes Road.

The Granville Theatre was built on part of the old green's triangular site. Founded by the music-hall artist Dan Leno, and designed by the prolific theatre architect Frank Matcham, it provided entertainment in a red-plush setting; it had a brief revival in the 1950s when Ellen Pollock presented a season of *Grand Guignol* theatre there. It was finally demolished in 1971.

Walham Green was also lavishly supplied with early 'picture palaces'. These included the Walham Green Cinematograph Theatre at 583 Fulham Road, the Broadway Gardens (behind the station), Fulham Picture Palace (later the Ritz) at 260 North End Road, another at 344 North End Road, and the Fulham Electric Theatre at no. 303. Another, opposite the Granville in Fulham Road, was known as 'Pike's Circuit', and there was also the Red Hall which became the Walham Green Gaumont.

Walham Green also had seven pubs. Apart from the George there was the Red Lion, the King's Head, the White Hart, the Swan, the Maltsters and the Cock. In North End Road were the Jolly Brewer, the Norfolk Arms (now demolished), and the Crown, now the Fulham Tap. (Sadly, modern names have supplanted some of the ancient ones lately – The King's Head has become the Slug and Lettuce, and the Red Lion is now a Bar Grill.) Charles Fèret was impressed by the rebuilding of the Cock in the 1890s with its saloon bar

67. The King's Head, Walham Green. From a watercolour made by a child in 1810.

68. The Old Cock, 1894.

decorated with palms and other plants.

By 1902 Fulham had bowed to the demand for a public baths and wash-house. This was built opposite the church and found its supporters even as late as 1979 when the Council wanted to close it on the grounds of safety. A 'Save Our Baths' group, led by Alice Davies, organised a petition of 14,000 names, a march to Hammersmith Town Hall and a sit-in at the baths which was to last over a year before a High Court action evicted them. The battle was lost and the new baths, without laundry facilities, and now known as Fulham Pools, was opened in the 1980s on a site adjacent to the old Normand House.[5]

'This bit of old Fulham has fallen on evil days', said Fèret of Farm Lane in the 1890s. Rocque's map of 1741–45 showed no houses here and even in 1825 there were only three, High House, Wynyaw House and a laundry known as Pat's Power. Most of the land between here and Exeter Place was owned by the Whitbread brewing family in the 18th century, which sold five acres to John Stocken, son of the owner of the Swan Brewery. Stocken's house here was leased on his death by Samuel Walden, founder of the Peterborough Benevolent Society, an organisation begun at the Peterborough pub in 1833, to provide money and coals to poor local residents. In 1840 the Stocken family sold three acres of land in the vicinity to the Butchers' Charitable Institution, which built a row of Gothic-style almshouses here. By 1900 extensions provided homes for about 70 pensioners including the 'King of Walham Green' himself, the butcher John Knights, who had, presumably, fallen on harder times. In the grounds stood a pump (now in the Museum of London) which provided a living for a blind water-carrier who distributed to those who had no mains supply.

The site continued to be used for charitable purposes when the alms-

69. *Fulham Ladies' Swimming Baths, c1915.*

70. *The Butchers' Almshouses, south side, Vanston Place.*

71. The cover of Timothy Davies fashion catalogue in 1914.

72. Page from a Timothy Davies catalogue 1939.

houses moved out in 1900. Here the Samuel Lewis Trust built their large, recently modernised, blocks of low-cost housing.

Pictures of Fulham Broadway at the end of the last century show the newly-built Granville with its glass-covered canopy. The road is crowded with horse traffic, buses and brewers' drays as well as delivery carts. On the south side is the terrace of shops owned by the Liberal politician Timothy Davies, the Welsh draper, who opened his first shop here in 1885.[6] He liked to tell how he walked from South Kensington to Walham Green to investigate the prospects at Fulham Broadway when only two shops were completed, one of which he took, and which expanded later to take in the whole terrace. He was later to be mayor of Fulham and its first Liberal MP.

The King's Head is recorded by 1680. It was a popular venue for parties which strolled to it from Fulham and Chelsea to enjoy its tea garden. The White Hart, opposite, has even earlier origins, being noted in the Churchwardens' accounts of 1632, when payment was made for a 'poor minister lying sick there'.

Just behind the White Hart, where stood Elton Villa, the Vestry acquired the site for the new Town Hall of 1890, designed by George Edwards.

The Wesleyans came to Fulham via the zeal of members of Sloane Terrace Chapel in Chelsea, some of whom established a Salem Chapel at Walham Green. The Metropolitan Railway needed a large part of the chapel's site for what was then called Walham Green Station and the Methodists erected a new building nearby. Some old Broadway houses may still be seen in the terrace between the station and the chapel, where shops stand on the old front gardens. In one of these buildings the artist Henri Gaudier Brzeska lived from 1891–1915.

In the early years of this century the impresario, Sir Oswald Stoll, made no less than six attempts to persuade the authorities to grant him a licence to open a music hall in Fulham Road, all of which were refused on the grounds that a sufficient number of these establishments already drew crowds of undesirables to the area.[7] During the 1st World War Stoll decided to build instead an estate of flats for disabled ex-servicemen on his site, Oswald Stoll Mansions, which has inscribed on its main gates the famous battles of the Great War.

Across the road, at about the same time, the Lord Roberts Memorial Workshops of the Soldiers, Sailors and Airmen's Families Association were established in a handsome main building in Waterford Road, with a factory behind. The former is now used as DHSS offices and the latter has been sold off for private development, the capital being used to further the charity's work: a history of these workshops is recorded on the wall of the new buildings.

Only three of the handsome early Victorian villas (out of about twenty) remain in the stretch of road leading to Stamford Bridge stadium. Known collectively as Stamford Villas,[8] the residents included Napoleon III and Hablot Knight Browne, better known as the book illustrator 'Phiz'. Happily, a developer has not destroyed the Italian Village. Hidden behind a high wall, this is approached by a heavy wooden door, leading to a secret garden, and a wrought-iron arch commemorating its architect, Mario Manenti (1885–1954). A group of small, red tile-roofed houses looks out onto garden courtyards and archwayed paths, so charming that one hesitates to record it for fear that it should be betrayed. The Italian Village adjoins another group of studios created out of what were once workshops for musical instrument makers. Behind one studio is a magnificent fig tree, said to be 300 years old and the most ancient in England.

The councillors who were fearful of the effect Stoll's music hall may have had on the decorum of Fulham Broadway did not anticipate the more traumatic advent of Chelsea Football Club at Stamford Bridge. The Club (actually in Fulham rather than Chelsea), founded in 1905 by Joseph Mears, has had a

73. North End Road market, c1904.

colourful history, marred in recent years by very bad crowd trouble. Recently, controversial plans for the development of the ground, along with that of Fulham Football Club, have caused much rancour.[9] These proposals are still unresolved and it remains to be seen if the stadium will be redeveloped entirely for other uses or else still provide a home for the club.

The market along North End Road stemmed from the King's Road costers, and other traders from Hammersmith, being moved from their pitches by the lobbying of shopkeepers. North End Road was to gain financially and it was one of the highlights of the area late on Saturday nights when the market was still flourishing. Nowadays the high street names occupy the shops which surround the market traders. Gone are the Welsh drapers A.B. Williams and Tudor Jones and even the family firm of F.H. Barber is much reduced in size. The market traders themselves are still family concerns; many of them have intermarried and out of this network of relatives and friends has developed a stability which enables them to know their customers over many years and to withstand efforts to shift the market elsewhere. Lately, many of the pitches have been taken over by people selling clothes and jewellery, which is not popular with the old traders, but the market still has an earthy, fruity flavour. Despite a bit of roguishness the traders display much kindness to those who find shopping physically difficult or to those who simply don't have much money.

One large house, which existed in this area until 1881, was Shorrolds (a name which stemmed from the Sherwold family in medieval times). It was of plain brick, set in two acres planted, it was said, with every tree and shrub

74. The 25-miles race for the Amateur Bicycle Championship at Lillie Bridge. From The Graphic, *6 February, 1875.*

which can be grown in the open air – once again, Fulham is identified with horticulture. Facing Walham Grove was North End Lodge, occupied until 1860 by an entertainer called Albert Richard Smith, whose diorama of Mont Blanc drew large crowds to the Egyptian Hall in Piccadilly.

One old business which survives in North End Road is the monumental masons of T. Crowther, its lower floor obscured by a café, but its trade proclaimed by a monumental lion on the roof.

The Victorian building of the Jolly Brewer survives at the corner with Haldane Road, as does the Fulham Tap, near Lillie Road junction, rebuilt in 1879. The latter has previously been called the Crown and the Fulham Volunteer.

On the east side of North End Road stood a house called Copt Hall (later the Grange) in six and a half acres of grounds. It had two storeys with low-beamed ceilings and panelled rooms and was at one time occupied by Charles Batty, a builder who developed much of northern and central Fulham. Eustace and Armadale Roads occupy the site. At the corner of Eustace Road until the late 1950s was Dell's, a grain-merchant selling loose barley, oats, chicken feeds, spices and the like; its proprietor, who dressed in long-skirted tweeds of Victorian design, was said to be the sister of the romantic novelist, Ethel M. Dell. The shop is now a travel agency.

Going north from here towards Lillie Road the streets were built on swampy ground called Marshcroft, which could be flooded by a high tide at Chelsea Creek. Beaufort House, near the Lillie Road junction, was built in this area in the early part of the 19th century; this later became a private mental asylum and was latterly the headquarters of the South Middlesex Rifle Volunteers with a rifle range in the grounds. It was demolished in 1904 and an LCC school built on the site.

On the south-east corner of Lillie Road and North End Road a large and impressive Carmelite nunnery was built in 1880. The order was a strict one: the nuns never left the convent and no visitors were allowed except for those outsiders who attended worship in the chapel, but even then the nuns were screened from their view. Its life was short – barely twenty years – before being replaced by a shop terrace.

The eastern end of Lillie Road was planned by Sir John Lillie in 1826. It included the North End Brewery, established in 1832, and a terrace of houses, Rosa Villas, many of which still remain on the north side. These included one with an elaborate coat-of-arms over the door, said to be the work of an architectural plasterer to the royal household, Joseph Bickley. This same house also has a Gothic style studio at the bottom of its secluded garden, with a legendary association with Edward VII and Lily Langtry. The largest enterprise in the vicinity was that of the London Roadcar Company, one of the biggest proprietors of horse-drawn buses in London; their stables and yards covered the whole distance between Seagrave Road, originally a service road to the railway depots and works, and Farm Lane.

The marshy ground on either side of the Creek escaped development but in the 1860s and '70s the site was ideal for the establishment of large recreational facilities. The Lillie Bridge Athletic Grounds were opened in March 1869, and the London Athletic Club was established in 1876 on a site later to be that of the Chelsea Football Club. A poster advertising an event at Lillie Bridge in 1875 announces 'Great Feats of Strength and Foot Racing. Catch-hold Wrestling, Rope Pulling in Gangs, a One Mile Flat race, Putting a 16 pound weight and racing a wheel barrow carrying 2cwt for 50 yards.[10]

On the east side of Seagrave Road was established in 1877 the Fulham Smallpox Hospital on land bought from the Kensington Board of Guardians. Subsequently it catered for other infectious diseases such as scarlet fever and diphtheria, and it was renamed the Western Fever Hospital. When it was

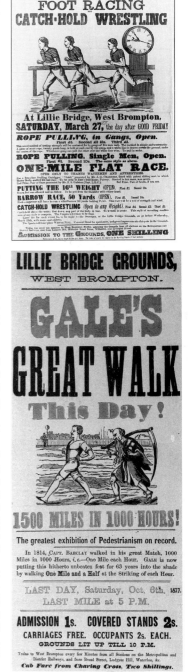

75. *Various sporting events advertised at the Lillie Bridge ground in 1875.*
76. *Gales Great Walk at the Lillie Bridge ground, 1877.*

enlarged in 1896–98 it was stipulated that no building occupied by patients should be within 1000 feet of the Butchers' Almshouses at Walham Green, for fear of infection. After the last war the Western became a chest hospital and then was made redundant. On its site is now a housing development called Brompton Park Crescent which includes a garden, swimming pool, gymnasium and other leisure facilities, but the old ambulance station in Seagrave Road, now rebuilt as one the world's largest, has been retained.

The rival village of Walham Green is still changing. Here and there, what was an old house or two, a redundant factory, or a railway yard, are lost when the wraps of temporary hoardings are taken down to reveal new houses, a modern mews or some other development. A towering hotel overshadows the studios hidden behind Seddlescombe Road, the maze of taxi and other garages in Farm Lane becomes a complex of small businesses. Now the proposal of a new arterial road, the Western Environmental Improvement Route, along the line of the railway, presents a new threat of disruption, much resented by many inhabitants. Latest developments indicate that this has now been indefinitely postponed.

NOTES ON SOURCES

1 Lysons, p257; Feret, Vol II, pp241–242.
2 Feret, Vol II, pp209–211.
3 *Ibid.*, Vol II, p217.
4 *Ibid.*, Vol II, pp234–239.
5 *Fulham Chronicle* files 1979–81.
6 Hasker, p118.
7 *Ibid.*, pp153–156 and 163.
8 Feret, Vol II, p216.
9 *Fulham Chronicle* and *Fulham Times*, 1985 onwards.
10 *Life in Fulham*, (Hammersmith and Fulham Libraries 1985), p1.

CHAPTER EIGHT

Nightingales at Sands End

It is over 200 years since Joseph Addison, the 18th-century journalist, wit, politician and scholar, heard the nightingale sing at Sands End in Fulham, recording the occasion in a letter from his country retreat there to his pupil, the young Earl of Holland and Warwick.[1] Now there may be blackbirds whistling bravely above the roar of the the diesel lorries rumbling over Wandsworth Bridge, even a lone heron flapping lazily across the mud flats of the river at low tide, but nothing else is left of this once-rural corner of Fulham. It is now the territory of tomorrow as developers move into the riverside area which the Victorians despoiled.

Sands End stretches from the Creek which divides Fulham from Chelsea, to the old Peterborough estate on the west side of Wandsworth Bridge Road. The river is its boundary to the south and the King's Road is its northern edge. Fifty years ago it was even uglier than it is today, but thriving, with a huge gasworks and power station, an oil depot, laundry, and various other factories. But by the 1970s it had become a dead and derelict industrial wasteland, the power station unused, the gasometers either deflated or demolished, factories empty and the corner shops closed. In once-busy Townmead Road there was little traffic other than the occasional oil tanker, and a man on a bike, familiar in the factory days, was a rare sight.

Close up, the chimney stacks of the dormant power station seemed enormous. Each was three hundred feet high, crowning an already high building. An inscription above the main door 'Fulham Borough Council, Electricity Department', is a reminder that a number of borough councils pioneered the supply of electricity.[2] Fulham built their first power station here in 1901 but the immense building which has recently been demolished was not opened until 1936. Part of its site has been used for a Sainsbury's supermarket, while developers have plans to fill the rest of the riverside area with a sports complex, offices and homes.

The surrounding streets have undergone renovation but most of the corner shops, such as Mr Turner's greengrocery smelling of boiled beetroots, and Ockenden's the newsagents, have gone or are boarded up and sprayed or chalked with graffiti. The Roman Catholic Church of Our Lady of Perpetual Succour, built in 1922, survives on the corner of Stephendale Road, and provides some continuity. It is a large, grey building, somewhat Flemish in appearance, with a green copper-tipped tower.

Of all the parts of Fulham, Sands End has the fewest reminders of rurality. Could Bagley's Lane really be named from the owner of orchards here? But by 1900 Charles Fèret was lamenting that 'soon it will no longer be possible to stroll out to the country' this way.[3] There were, he said 'two or three genteel streets leading towards the newly-built Wandsworth Bridge Road', but the rest has become 'a region of poverty and squalor' – this of a place which only fifty years earlier had been a pretty riverside mead growing watercresses, with cows wading into the stream and no more traffic than an occasional cart.

Sands End may be named from the sandy banks of the outlet of the Creek, or from its earliest recorded landowner, John de Saundeford, in the reign of Edward I.[4] Henry VIII granted the manor of Sandford to the Abbot of Westminster, but the land returned to the Crown in 1549; Mary I sold it about ten years later to a London mercer, William Maynard. Residents, first noted at the end of Elizabeth's reign, were few, even by the middle of the 17th century, because the land was marshy and suitable only for pasture. By the side of the river were fields recalling the very rural days – Owl Acre, Elm Tree Field, Dock Mead (once famous for osiers). At the Chelsea end, where the fields were laced with watercourses and ditches and flanked by an embankment to withstand the high tides, other names included Inmead, Wild Mead, le Strode and Peresterse. Tenants were allowed to let loose a fixed number of cattle to graze on these meadows after Lammas Day (August 1).[5]

Early in the 19th century the three most easterly fields, Frogmill Bank, Fan Mead and Wild Mead, were the site of a canal devised by William Edwardes, the third Lord Kensington, who was anxious to bring trade to his estate in Kensington. A two-mile channel, a hundred feet wide, was proposed, to carry vessels of up to a hundred tons from the river just below Lacey's Point to a basin situated roughly on the line of the present Pembroke Road, Kensington. Part of Fan Mead was sold to him and other investors, compensation being paid to the William Powell Almshouses who derived some of their income from the land. By the time the almshouses got their money, twenty years later, the canal had been abandoned and sold to the West London Railway Company as a route for a new line. Later, this was extended across the river to connect with the South London Railway tracks at Clapham Junction. Once railway lines occupied the Frog and Fan Meads, the osiers withered, and the king cups and watercresses were replaced by persistent ragworts and buddleias amongst the sleepers and cinders.

But development of this area was the subject of much controversy. Two separate small parts of the meads belonged to the parish – a bequest of 1491. Proceeds from the produce went towards the church rate, but they were of little account, amounting to only about £9 in 1802, and in 1883 the Trustees sold the land to the Imperial Gas Company. Aware then of the financial return that these previously desolate marshes would bring, the Vestry promoted a Bill in Parliament which would either ensure that the land was used as an open space or else, when sold, provide revenue to open a park elsewhere. But already owners of the various meads had been fencing round what they thought was their property, thereby depriving the tenants of grazing rights. The Vestry assembled a number of workmen and accompanied by the police, broke down one enclosure and led a token number of horses in to graze. It all ended in the High Court where, in February 1893, the judge awarded in the owners' favour. The Lammas rights were gone forever.

All that remains of the old manor is, surprisingly, the manor house, itself becoming a matter of argument between those who favoured conservation or demolition. The house, so legend has it (here, and in many places besides!), was once occupied by Nell Gwynne. This is conjecture without evidence, but the discovery of a thimble bearing the initials 'N.G.' and a Freemason's badge, or jewel, supposedly owned by Charles II (later presented to the Lodge of the gas engineer who found it), has added fuel to the belief. In the *Domestic Intelligencer* of 5 August 1679, is a report of an incident when 'Madame Ellen Gwynne's mother, sitting lately by the waterside at her house by the neat houses near Chelsey, fell accidentally into the water and was drowned.' A row of cottages nearby which lined the path to the Manor House, were named for Nell Gwynne, and perpetuated the legend.[6]

Stanley Bridge, the last of the four Fulham bridges over the boundary creek, was known earlier as Stone or Bull Bridge, the latter from a hostelry which stood on its western side. The essayist, Richard Steele, founder of *The Tatler*, addressed a letter to his wife there in August 1710, arranging to meet her. The inn is no more and only historic records recall the trees which surrounded it with seats on which travellers could rest.

The residence of Joseph Addison at Sands End, unlike that of Mistress Gwynne, is supported by documentary evidence. He wrote many letters from here and Jonathan Swift, in his *Journal to Stella*, mentions Addison's retirement near Chelsea. Two years earlier, in 1708, Addison wrote to the young Earl of Warwick and Holland, Henry Rich, (whose mother he was patiently wooing) a letter headed 'Sandy End, Fulham'. 'I want', it said, 'to invite you to a concert of music which I have found in a neighbouring wood. It consists of a blackbird, a thrush, a robin redbreast and a bull finch. There is a lark by the way of an overture, the whole is concluded by a nightingale...'

In 1762 the manor house became a factory for the production of saltpetre and in 1790 a German, James Ruel, transferred his pottery business here from Chelsea. This occupation was again shortlived and other businesses followed in the house, such as clothmaking and cask manufacture. The latter concern was evidently on hard times in December 1818, for the owner issued a circular explaining a plan to relieve the distress of the poor in that coming winter (it was the time of Peterloo – one of much poverty and hardship). He says that his warehouse and workshops in which 200–300 people were normally employed were 'unoccupied owing to the generally depressed state of the trade, but possessed an unqualified capacity for being rendered fit for the comfortable accommodation of a very considerable number of poor persons'. He promised to provide them with 'every necessary article of wholesome provision and convenience for sleeping'. In return they would be employed in bundling and cutting firewood for sale to the public at a reduced price. This venture, supported by the Bishop of London, lasted only a few months until March 1819, when the factory began work on the production of wooden canteens for soldiers.

77. Sandford Manor House. Oil by J. Widmer.

78. Joseph Addison.

79. Construction of No. 6 gasholder in 1880.

The Sandford Manor estate, with the house itself, was bought by the Imperial Gas Light & Coke Company in 1824. Here, next to the river where the coal barges unloaded, the Company established one of its major works; the manor house was used as housing for senior employees. The oldest working gasholder in the world is now the only one which survives and it is guarded by a Preservation Order. At the time of its construction it was an innovation. Most holders of this period had a capacity of about 40,000 cubic feet, but this one, designed by Samuel Clegg, held 250,000 cubic feet. Additional holders included one built in 1867 with a capacity of 2,500,000 cubic feet, nicknamed 'The Sultan' following a visit by the Shah of Persia in 1873. He was so impressed by what he saw that he concluded that its designer, named Murdoch, must have been a reincarnation of Merdoch, the Assyrian god of light, and accordingly ordered him to be canonised.

Apart from providing work for hundreds of local inhabitants, the gas works played an important part in the development of this part of Fulham. Imperial Road, parallel to Bagleys Lane, was created as the result of negotiations between the gas company and Fulham District Board of Works, when the former wanted to extend its works across Sand End Lane. The company paid for the new road plus £1000 compensation.

A sideline of the manufacture of gas and coke was the production of low-gravity gas for ballooning. In April 1908 a special mile-long pipe was laid to the Hurlingham Club grounds where 31 balloonists competed in an international contest.[7]

Imperial Road and Square were built by the Company; the latter, of 1880, for gasworks staff, is a hidden oasis of greenery and two-storey cottages off

80. The modern restoration of Sandford House.

Imperial Road. It became known as 'German Square', the story being that during a strike a number of Germans and Russians were imported to keep the works running and the cottages were built to house them. Certainly there were many German families living in Fulham at the turn of the century – enough to justify a Lutheran church in Kelvedon Road.

The introduction of North Sea gas made the works redundant. In the 1980s the Square and the surrounding area were bought by the local council and the Square refurbished. Meanwhile, in 1972, the manor house and other lands were sold to Romulus Construction Co. and for the next 16 years, as the area lay dormant or used for breaking up old cars, surrounded by corrugated iron fences, the house was the subject of a sustained campaign by conservation groups – it was not until 1987 that restoration began in conjunction with English Heritage and Hammersmith and Fulham Council. The house, restored to its former glory and retaining many of its original features, but adapted for business use, was formally opened by Lord Montagu of Beaulieu, Chairman of English Heritage, in March 1989.[8]

Only one non-industrial relic of the rural past, other than Sandford Manor, survives and this is a mid 19th-century rebuilding of a much earlier residence. This is Grove House in Bagleys Lane, which John Bowack, author of *Antiquities of Middlesex* and a resident of Sands End Lane from 1730, described in 1786 as 'a very ancient seat…sweetly situated and very pleasant in summer although in winter sometimes incommoded by the water, being on low ground. The gardens are extraordinarily fine and many wintergreens [evergreens] such as cypress, yew and fir which flourish here extremely well, make it remarkable.' This house, occupied from 1763 to 1812 by four generations of the Smith family all with the christian name of Deliverance, passed eventually to the market gardening family of Bagley. During their time 35 acres were planted with fruit and nuts.

The industrialisation of Sands End, begun by the gasworks in 1824, was further encouraged by the opening of Wandsworth Bridge in 1873. Stanford's map of 1892 shows a chemical factory and a 'tile works' by Townmead Road. The latter appears to be a prosaic description of the pottery that William De Morgan opened in 1888 in association with the architect Halsey Ricardo, who pioneered the use of tiles on the exterior of houses to combat the dirt and corrosion of the London atmosphere. De Morgan, of course, is famed for his beautiful pottery decorated with birds, flowers and fishes in bright greens, blues and reds, all with strong Persian and Turkish influences; he also experimented with the lustres used in Spanish and Moroccan ceramics. One of his largest commissions, the Arab Room at Leighton House, Kensington, still survives. De Morgan's health broke down in 1908 and the pottery closed; the works, with its 70 foot kiln chimney, was converted into a factory producing metal polish, and then demolished to build the local authority estate, Coomber House.

Another large industrial concern was Van der Bergh's margarine factory, here from the turn of the century until 1934. The Sunlight Laundry was established in Broughton Road in 1900, and MacFarlane Lang made biscuits in Townmead Road. Kops Brewery was established on the Meads as early as 1890: its vast, gloomy building in Townmead Road is now a warehouse and depot. Next door Fulham Vestry opened a depot where refuse was loaded on to barges.

Despite the nearness of industry quite select streets of his 'lion' houses were built by Jimmy Nichols on either side of Wandsworth Bridge Road. St Matthew's church, on the corner of Rosebury Road, was consecrated in 1895 and a public library opposite was provided the following year. A chapel-of-ease in those days of assiduous church-going was opened in Townmead Road – this survives as a youth centre, lurid with mural graffiti, but still bearing its inscription 'To the glory of God…'.

Remarkably, this area has been chosen for an expensive development – Chelsea Harbour. Twenty acres of coal yards were bought by P & O and Globe in the 1980s to produce what they described as a 'unique world of houses, flats, offices, restaurants and shops', and a luxury hotel built around a working yacht harbour. There is a vast underground car park, a river bus service to the City and Docklands, and the central Belvedere Tower is topped by a tidal ball which gauges the height of the tide. The architecture contains a mixture of classical and modernistic styles and motifs, much in the style of Docklands, and although the prices are high the development is not exclusive – the general public can enjoy its amenities, including the riverside walk which will be extended from Wandsworth to Chelsea. In such ways London is reclaiming its riverside and such schemes echo the dream of Sir Patrick Abercrombie, author of the Greater London Plan in 1943, who envisaged such a riverside path as well as the opening of the grounds of Fulham Palace and Hurlingham to the public.

But what might be considered a prestigious improvement to this once down and out corner of old Fulham, received a chilly welcome from the local authority, which proposed to the Boundaries Commission that the Chelsea Harbour area be redesignated to Kensington and Chelsea on the eastern side of the railway line. 'We do appreciate that perhaps a 100 years ago Chelsea Creek formed a natural boundary that would put Chelsea Harbour with us but that argument is no longer the case', a Hammersmith and Fulham Council spokeswoman was quoted in the *Kensington and Chelsea Times* in February 1988. 'Logically it should be administered by Kensington and Chelsea'. Hammersmith and Fulham Council had granted planning permission for the development at its inception, but that was in the days of a Conservative majority, shortly afterwards overturned by Labour. The offer of the additional 20 acres aroused no enthusiasm on the other side of the border where the Council leader of the time, Nicholas Freeman, said 'The Royal Borough had completed its submissions to the Boundaries Commission. No suggestion that we should take Chelsea Harbour into this authority was among them. That will remain our position.'

Rumour in the political corridors is that the Labour controlled Hammersmith and Fulham Council does not welcome the large influx of potentially Tory voters in the previously safe Labour ward of Sands End, plus the additional Poll Tax work, a tax, which unlike the old rating system, takes no account of increased property values.

Equally controversial is the plan for a new arterial road, the Western Environmental Improvement Route (WEIR), which would impose many changes on the Townmead area, involving the demolition of property.

NOTES ON SOURCES

1   Feret, Vol III, pp273–274.
2   Hasker, pp143, 156, 173, 174, 179, 186, 194, 199, 201.
3   Feret, Vol II, p82.
4   Feret, Vol III, pp268, 269.
5   Feret, Vol III, pp256, 257, 260.
6   'Fulham's Romantic Past' in *Co-Partners' Magazine*, November 1937, published by the Gas Light & Coke Company; *Thames Gas Magazine*, July 1945; Feret, Vol III, p273.
7   *Co-Partners' Magazine*, September 1911, p135, published by the Gas Light & Coke Company; *Historical Index of Gas Works, 1806–1957*, p41.
8   *Hammersmith and Fulham Times*, 17 March 1989. Romulus Construction bought the estate in 1971 and, after lengthy negotiations with English Heritage and the local authority, developed the surrounding land for low rent housing. At the same time they carried out careful restoration of the manor house. The structure was reinforced with concealed steel columns, the tiled floor and panelling were made good, and the seven-flight staircase and the Elizabethan chimneys were rebuilt.

CHAPTER NINE

In Fulham Fields

Fulham Fields in mid–18th century maps denoted the area roughly between Lillie and Fulham Roads; later, this sparsely inhabited agricultural and horticultural acreage included land further north towards the Hammersmith boundary.

Two main highways crossed the Fields. They were the Church Way from the hamlet of Hammersmith (which had no church of its own until the building of a chapel-of-ease in the 1630s) running parallel with the river (now Fulham Palace Road), and Fulham Road, which was the road to London. Two minor roads ran west to east, Paynes or Crown Lane (now Lillie Road) and Parys Lane, along the line of today's Dawes Road.

The first mention of the London Road from old Fulham High Street (or Bere Street) to Walham or Wedens greene (Fulham Broadway) can be found in records of 1442. By the 18th century this narrow, unmade-up lane, flanked on both sides by fields and market gardens, was increasingly popular as a residential area for those tired of crowded and insanitary inner London, but even so late as 1867 old photographs show the London Road as a rural lane with fences and shrubbery on either side and few buildings.

The first estate on the northern side of the road at its junction with Fulham High Street and the way to Hammersmith, was Holcrofts House or Hall,[1] built on land named from a Tudor family; in 1700 the distinguished Fulham merchant, Robert Limpany, bought the estate and built a new house on it, which survived until the 1890s. He didn't live in it long. Within a few years his cousin, William Withers, later to be a Lord Mayor of London and a Whig MP for the City of London, bought it. Subsequent occupants included the Duke of Wellington's Engineer in the Peninsular War, Major Sir John Fox Burgoyne, whose love of theatricals may have led to the next tenant being the actor Charles Mathews, who was married to the actress Madame Vestris.

On the south side of the London (Fulham) Road, opposite Holcrofts, was the ancient estate known as Cleybrookes, the land having been owned by a family of that name from 1518 to 1626.[2] One of its members, Stephen Cleybrooke, was pardoned for murder in 1537, and his more mundane misdemeanours are reported in the Court Rolls of 1565, when it was ordered that his land be seized 'in forfeit for divers causes, contempts, offences and acts against the customs of the manor'. A later occupant was Edward Frewen, canopy-bearer at the coronation of James II, who was knighted before that monarch fled the country. It was the Frewen family which sold the house to Limpany across the road in 1732.

In the mid-1870s the developer-builders, Gibbs and Flew, set their sights on the Fulham Park Estate, which adjoined the Cleybrookes land, and included Fulham Lodge, described in 1804 as a 'compact and convenient detached villa with new-built coach house stables, billiard room, walled garden, pleasure ground, lawns, shrubberies, hot house and two meadows, containing altogether ten acres'.[3] One of its residents was Eliza Carey, an actress much admired by Frederick, Duke of York, of 'marching up and down' fame. When the house was sold in 1838 its attractions also included a laundry, a snug little cottage for a bachelor in the grounds and 'in a private place a hermitage fitted up in excellent taste'. After its demolition in the 1840s part of the ground was taken by a member of the Strand India Outfitters firm, Thresher Glenny, who built himself a new house just westward of the Dungannon nursery gardens owned by his brother, George, who advertised their Balsam seed as the best in the world. George, already well-known as a gardening journalist in his *Gardeners' Gazette* and *Gardening Almanac*, was one of the founders of the Gardeners' Royal Benevolent Institution.

Rivals to Glenny were the Dancers, a family which was late in switching from market to nursery gardening. Their land stretched along the southern side of Fulham Road, almost as far as today's St Dionis Road, and eastward to Park House on the corner of Parsons Green Lane. Proudly advertising their camelias and conifers, this family of four generations retained the firm until 1880. A forebear, Nathaniel Dancer, had, in 1657, left a sum of twenty shillings a year to be spent from the income of two acres of land at Fulham Park House, to provide meat and bread to poor people at Christmas and for a sermon from the Vicar of Fulham on January 1 for ever.[4]

A later nursery in this part of the Fields was that of Thomas and Charles Lockhart who were renowned for their hyacinths, most of which were imported from Holland. They went bankrupt in 1840 when 200,000 bulbs, greenhouses and stocks of seeds were sold.

In the story of Munster Road, the small main road which now provides one of the few north-south 'rat-runs' through Fulham, a benefactor with an assumed name, a mad doctor and a romantic duchess, play leading roles.[5] Munster Lane, as it was then called, is mentioned in the Court Rolls of Fulham as early as the reign of Henry VII, but it was not until 1832 that this byway continued beyond Fulham Road to New King's Road. Munster House (which actually fronted Fulham Road rather than Munster Road) dominated the Munster area.[6] It was a long, three-storey building surrounded by eight acres, much older than the castellations which decorated it in later days. In 1705 the historian John Bowack described it as a 'handsome ancient house' and its occupants may be traced back to the reign of Charles I when a member of the Powell family, already landowners in Fulham, lived there.[7] It was his nephew, William, who was obliged to adopt the name Powell in order to secure the inheritance, and who founded the almshouses and the school so long established in Fulham.

The romantic association of 'Munster' with the mistress of George I, the Duchess of Munster in Germany, Ehrengarde von Schulenberg, has been scotched by the fact that she was never rated for any property in Fulham and certainly never lived at Munster House.

The house became, in 1751, an asylum 'for the reception of gentlemen and ladies and others afflicted with nervous or melancholy disorders' and its gardens were described as 'well laid out for the amusement of persons under such unhappy circumstances.' Some forty years later the house became a school, reverted to a private residence, and then in 1849 became a lunatic asylum again, run by a Mr Cyrus Elliott and his brother Dr William Elliott; Cyrus eventually became insane himself and was confined in his own institution. It was William Elliott who installed the Gothic frontage and battlements, and at that time the establishment boasted 'eight acres of pleasure gardens studded with noble trees, lawns, meadows and orchards, a bowling green and bowling alley, with billiard and reading rooms and a padded room and refractory ward thus doing away with mechanical restraint'.[8] Feret's history of Fulham includes photographs of a grotto in the grounds of Munster House, which ended its days as a morgue for the asylum. He also mentions that the house was alive with droves of rats and mice which could be heard careering around at night.

The status of the southern leg of Munster Road must have slumped in the

81. Munster House, c1850.

1880s when the Vestry located its new dustcart depot there, adjacent to the railway bridge. There could hardly be a more illuminating example of the changing patterns of modern life than that the site of the old depot, cleared in the 1980s, is being used for one of the area's more luxurious developments, Mustow Close (thereby reviving the more ancient form of the word Munster); this is a group of high priced mews-type houses, near to the railway viaduct which once disturbed only the horses' slumber.

Vine Cottage, sited in the south-east corner of what is now Winchenden Road, was used by Wilkie Collins as the model for 'Salt Patch' in his novel *Man and Wife*;[9] he gave a detailed description of it, including its bell turret. Nearby was Westfield House, which became a public library in the 1880s, but was demolished so that a purpose-built library could succeed it. In that first library strict silence was enforced, and books were on a closed access system.

Probably the oldest surviving buildings in this section of the Fulham Road are two adjoining houses, Percy Villa and St Peter's Villa, both built in the 1840s and now incorporated in the Marist Convent School.

At the eastern end of Fulham Road, from Parsons Green to the Broadway, the area was once called Percy or Pursers Cross. Henry Hallam, historian and essayist, lived at Arundel House, (Kelvedon Road area), at the beginning of the 19th century.[10] Numerous literary friends visited him here, among which was the young Alfred Tennyson, who formed an ardent friendship with the historian's eldest son, Arthur Henry Hallam, and whose sudden death in 1833 inspired Tennyson's *In Memoriam*. Fèret thought the back of this house was most picturesque and described its 'quaint turret and old fashioned porch.' During repair work here the remains of a Tudor mansion were found and along the east wall a lead cistern bearing an earl's coronet and monogram, and the date 1703. It was demolished in 1898.

Dawes Road was formerly Parys Lane; it followed a devious way from Fulham Cross to the southern end of North End Road. Simon Parys was the owner of a large estate on the south-east side in the 14th century,[11] and the name of the lane features frequently in manorial records. It remained scarcely inhabited until the 19th century. Then we know of a baker's shop at the North End Road end, and it was here that the last parish beadle, a Mr Griffin, was born. It was also here that the first Fulham post office was established. Samuel Groves, the shoemaker next door to Griffin in the early years of the 19th century, gave a large plot of land called the Wastelands on the corner of Estcourt Road, to be used for 'new almshouses' despite much protest from local residents who would lose grazing rights on the land. The inhabitants of the almshouses were initially seven poor married couples, but the building was later extended to take in seven single people as well. The dwellings consisted of two rooms, each with a small yard and wash house, and the residents received pensions of up to eight shillings a week for a couple, with two sacks of coal each Christmas.

In modern times the most sensational association with Dawes Road stemmed from the activities of John George Haigh, the 'acid bath' murderer of the late 1940s. In 1947 Haigh met Archibald Henderson, a debonair doctor and his wife, Rose, a smart and beautiful woman, who had a toy shop and dolls' hospital at no. 16 Dawes Road. Haigh murdered both of them at his own workshop in Crawley and by clever forgeries obtained over £7,000 of their assets. Then, with typical coolness, he destroyed their bodies in a bath of acid, and took over the care of their dog and the answering of their correspondence.[12]

Gibbs and Flew, the builder-developers of the Fulham Park estate, also built the 'Salisbury' estate here, centred around the Salisbury Hotel public house. When this and the St John's Farm estate, covering an area around Goaters Alley and Homestead Road, were developed, the Parys estate was rural no longer.

Churches followed the developments. St Peter's, in Varna Road, was opened in 1882. The Roman Catholics had opened St Thomas's, in Rylston Road, in 1847 – the funds for building this were supplied by Elizabeth Bowden, who also founded St Thomas's Schools.[13] The church has interior decorations by Pugin and a 142ft spire. The Bowdens lived in Mulgrave House, Hurlingham: Mulgrave Road, off Lillie Road, is a reminder of the family's generosity to Fulham.

82. St Thomas's church, from the Illustrated London News, *1857.*

Of the school which Elizabeth Bowden began, the LCC Schools Inspector wrote in November 1903: 'This is a successful school; the children are happy, spontaneous and natural'. The school log books, still preserved, paint a vivid picture of Fulham schooldays in Victorian days. In 1897 it is recorded that 'the Infants School is overcrowded, the present staff is insufficient for 230 children and there are 340 on the books, some of the classes are seven desks deep...in the Babies Room a pupil teacher is teaching 51 children'. In 1901: 'Today a boy, Frank Read, was taken seriously ill in school, owing to his extreme weakness and pain it was impossible to send him home...the doctor came and pronounced him to be in a state of exhaustion and neglect owing to lack of food...this was communicated to his mother as soon as she returned from her work to her home.' Children were accepted at a very early age and there is a lament that certain three-year-olds had not yet learnt to read. We find, too, that 'boys have started to learn to thread needles' and, in 1888, 'most of the first class boys can knit, and all can sew'.

Nowadays, estate agents eulogise the Dawes Road area as being 'ideally situated to take advantage of all that London has to offer...with dozens of intimate bistros and wine bars...international airports easily accessible and Battersea Heliport only a mere cab drive away...' Charles Fèret could hardly have contributed such a flattering opinion of the area. When he wrote in the 1890s he dismissed Lillie Road with 'there is little to detain us here'. Certainly it was sparsely populated. There was a house on the site of the Normand Park Primary School and the Bramber Nursery, which was occupied in the 18th century by a family of German origin, the Weltjes, who were servants to the Prince Regent and his brother, Frederick, Duke of York. Normand House nestled behind a bank of trees, set back from the road, and approached by a driveway lined with elms.

The chapel on the corner of Tilton Street, now an evangelical Christian Fellowship, was originally founded as a Railway Mission by a Kensington benefactress, a Miss Eck, to serve the labouring gangs working on the railways nearby in the 1860s and 70s. The popular legend is that it is on the site of a plague pit.

Whatever else the Victorian poor lacked, it wasn't churches. Apart from the High Anglican church of St Augustine, consecrated in 1899 and destroyed during the blitz of World War II (it continues as a place of worship in a converted church hall), a large building at Fulham Cross where Lillie and Munster Roads meet, originally intended as a pub, was taken over in 1893 by the evangelist Sydney Black. He converted this into a Mission Chapel called Twynholm, with a small orphanage upstairs. Further along Lillie Road there was the Ebenezer Strict Baptist chapel, now taken over by an Indian sect.

These surviving places of worship and the old Halfway House pub are all that remain of 19th-century Fulham on this stretch of the north side of Lillie Road. The 'Bayonne Road development', a mix of Council and private development, now stretches north from Lillie Road to Greyhound Road. Some houses are rented, others owner-occupied, some in terraces and some grouped around a rather bare and depressing 'village green'. The neighbourhood library in the Clem Attlee estate replaced the Lillie Road branch opened in 1906.

The Recreation Ground, a triangular area of eight acres, was bought by the Vestry in 1891. In the 17th century it was the 'great orchard and gravel pits' belonging to the Lady Pye, mother of the merchant adventurer Nicholas Crispe, and was later known as Sandell's Corner, after the gardener's business there. Opposite the recreation ground is the Bishop Creighton House, named after a former Bishop of London, which began in 1908; after the 1st World War redundant munition workers were retrained here, and children from slum houses were sent on seaside holidays. The centre now looks after the needs of the elderly and handicapped.

Greyhound Road, originally Muscal Lane, follows the line of one of Fulham's most ancient byways, and is mentioned in the manor records as early as 1552. It takes its present name from a Victorian pub, established at the corner of Fulham Palace Road, the original of which was said to be so small that only three people could get into the bar, and whose roof was so low that almost anyone could reach up and touch it. It was popular with boxers and had a lively reputation, with races being run by the market girls, one of whom was found dead in a nearby ditch after a particularly riotous evening.

Nearby used to be a villa known as the Madman's House, the occupant of which lived on the top floors only, surrounded by stacks of plate and china. The site of this is now covered by Tasso Road, a cul-de-sac named for the free church Tabernacle founded here in 1887. In this road two of the area's old crafts survive – masons producing marble mantlepieces, and the Capricorn Iron-works, one of the few in London where wrought iron is forged on an original

83. The old Greyhound, demolished in 1882.

coke-fuelled furnace.

Greyhound Road, although now a popular 'rat run', might now have been an arterial road if a proposal in 1928 by the Society for Western Exits from London had materialised. This envisaged an offshoot to the Cromwell Road from North End Road via Greyhound Road, to a new bridge at Crabtree, a suggestion originally mooted by Fulham Council in 1913.

A great deal of post-war development has also occurred in the area of Margravine Road, where many of the small terraces had become slums and were knocked down before gentrification reached the area. The Anglican church of St Alban's began as a corrugated iron mission church in 1886 to take the overflow congregation from St Andrew's in Greyhound Road. Nearby is Baron's Court Cemetery, consecrated in 1869, whose peaceful acres provide one of the pleasantest open spaces in the borough, although the loss of an avenue of elms has given a bare aspect to the western entrance. Tottering angels, anchors, broken pillars and other Victorian bric-a-brac statuary are a reminder of death in the midst of life. At least the dead in the graves are identified, but in Greyhound Road, embedded into the wall of the Queen's Club, which came here in the 1880s, is a shrine, lacking part of its original inscription, but exhorting one to pray for... and then follow initials. The purpose of this memorial is not known, as it is undated and unrecorded.

The fertile soil of Fulham was said to have run out near its border with Hammersmith,[14] where the rich loam gave place to clay more suitable for making bricks than growing plants. The Chancellors of St Paul's Cathedral held a small manor in this remote corner of Fulham, a holding that extended into Hammersmith.[15] Between the two parishes ran Parrs Ditch, shown as 'Le Perre' in various court and ecclesiastical records.

The comparatively recent development of the land between Fulham Palace Road and the river is emphasised by Stanford's Map of the London Suburbs for 1892. In this the whole area between Distillery Lane and Bishops Avenue is shown as fields, crossed only by two lanes, Crabtree and Dorset, and a narrow footpath known as Crabtree Alley. Fulham Palace Road, or Church Way as it was called, was raised in status to that of a highway after the construction of the Fulham to Putney bridge, and in 1730 its upkeep was financed by tollgates. Yeldham Road was one of the first roads on the meadows on the other side of the road, where Monument Field lay. This field took its name from an obelisk erected in memory of his wife by the owner of one of the riverside mansions, George Bubb Dodington. It is said that the urn on its top contained the lady's heart, but in any case the obelisk was later re-erected by Lord Ailesbury of Tottenham, in Wiltshire, to celebrate the recovery from illness of George III.

At the corner of what is now St Dunstan's Road stood Sussex House, which had a conservatory and pleasure grounds; it was the home in 1808 of Prince Augustus Frederick, the sixth son of George III.[16] A later owner was Captain Frederick Marryat, the sailor-novelist whose tales, says Feret in 1900, 'delight our boys quite as much as they delighted their fathers a generation ago'. Marryat, born in 1792, ran away from school so many times that his father agreed to his joining the Navy at the age of fourteen. He had a distinguished service life and while living at Sussex House he wrote his novel *Jacob Faithful*, which is bound up with the history of the old Swan Inn. In 1844 the house was taken by Dr Forbes Benignus Winslow, a specialist in mental illness, who turned it into an asylum. He was also an enthusiast of phrenology, the study of the bumps on the head, and its relationship to mental instability.

Fulham built a new workhouse near Yeldham Road in 1850. It was Italian-ate in style, and within a year the number of inmates was about 550. In 1871 two new wings were added to provide infirmary space, and from this developed Fulham Hospital. But, in 1958, it was announced that a large new teaching hospital would be built here with the transfer from central London of Charing Cross Hospital. The *Fulham Chronicle* commented on the 'bitter indignation that has been aroused' by this announcement, and a Labour Party spokesman complained that there would be no guarantee that Fulham people would get priority in the new hospital.

The new Charing Cross Hospital, designed by Ralph Tubb, has 17 storeys, 900 beds and ten operating theatres, but despite its size (and its imported name) it has kept its local feeling and loyalty.

Fulham's last farm owner, William Matyear, whose family had been mar-ket gardeners in the area for a century or more, had the fields between the present Crabtree Lane and Colwith Road, and the last farmer was still growing his prize strawberries and cabbages when trams were running down Fulham Palace Road. At his death in 1910 he bequeathed his land to the King Edward VII Hospital Fund and it was sold by them for development. The purchasers, the developers Allen and Norris, were astute enough to take off the top twelve inches of fertile soil to sell to nurserymen.

Matyear's near neighbour on this southern boundary was the 'picturesque red brick pile' of the St James' Home for Female Penitents, a reformatory for female offenders, but only for those 'who by birth, education or inexperience of sin were considered superior to the common run of offender'. Established originally in Whetstone, Middlesex, with the support of St James' Church, Westminster, the home moved to Fulham when its out-of-London situation was considered inaccessible.

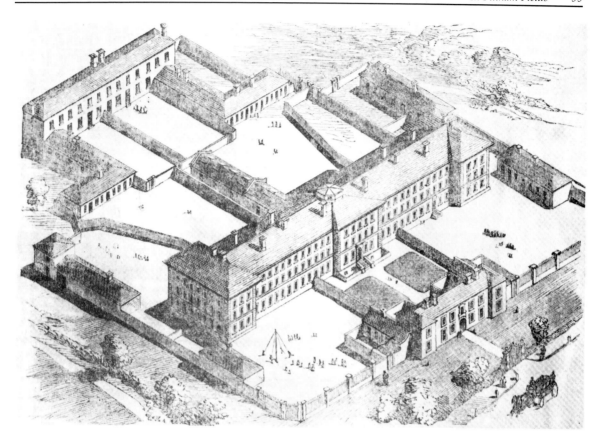

84. A birds-eye view of Fulham Union Workhouse. From the Illustrated London News, *1849.*

Fulham Cemetery, next to the Recreation Ground, was established for the same reason – the pressure of overcrowding – although this time for the dead. Originally consisting of just over five acres on the northern side, and consecrated by the Bishop of London in 1865, it was later enlarged to its eventual twelve acres. The first interment was that on the opening day, 3 August 1865, and the thirteenth that of a centenarian, Anne Salter, from Fulham Union Workhouse.

Just south of the Cemetery were the Lygon Almshouses, built in 1886 around three sides of a grassy square.[17] The land, known as the 'Lygon Acre', was bought for £900 by Lady Jemima Catherine Louisa Lygon in 1849, with the idea of building twelve almshouses to the memory of her brother and nephew. On hearing the scheme outlined the Bishop of London is said to have whispered to the Vicar 'Too beautiful to live', a remark overheard by the Lygon solicitor. This may have annoyed Lady Lygon, who did not proceed with her plan, but built her almshouses near Malvern instead. But the land *was* made over to the Charity Commissioners in trust for the parish of Fulham and used eventually for the almshouses built by the parish.

Fulham's mill stood on a piece of rising ground opposite the Lygon Almshouses.[18] It is not noted in the Domesday survey but it is mentioned often in 15th century records. The field was known as Millshot or Millfield, and part of what is now Fulham Palace Road also took the name of Mill Way or Windmill Worple. The mill was leased by the lord of the manor for terms of seven years or more. In the leases it was stipulated that if the miller ground the corn required

85. *In the workhouse dining room, c1905.*

86. *The Fulham workhouse post office, c1905.*

87. The dispensary of the Fulham Union Infirmary, 1912.

88. The operating theatre at the Fulham Union Infirmary, 1911.

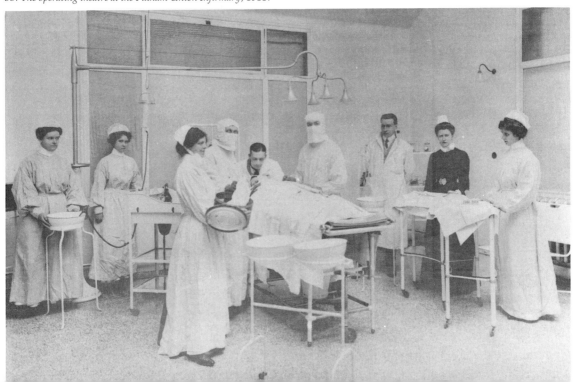

by the Bishop and his household, then rent should be reduced by the value of this service. The rent was usually paid in cash, but sometimes payment could be made in flour, salt or fish. The old structure was taken down about 1794.

The London Borough of Hammersmith and Fulham must be one of the few municipal authorities to claim three nationally known football clubs within its boundaries – Chelsea, Fulham and Queens Park Rangers.

Fulham Football Club was founded in 1879 by lads who attended the Sunday School at St Andrew's in Greyhound Road and its first matches as 'Fulham St Andrew's' were played on various grounds. It was not until 1896 that they acquired the derelict thatched Craven Cottage, which had been badly damaged by fire some eight years earlier. The new 'Cottage' pavilion-type building and the stand were not built until 1906 and it is they, as well as the affection for the club and its traditions, that have helped to save it from many development threats in the past decade. First there was a proposal to merge it with Queens Park Rangers, and there have been more plans, unresolved, since. The stand was designed by Archibald Leitch and both it and the Cottage are listed buildings.

The old church lads' team went professional in 1898 when the club joined the Southern League. Its finest hours were probably its promotion to the First Division in 1959 and its appearance in the Cup Final of 1975 with great names such as Johnny Haynes, Alan Mullery and Bobby Moore, under the management of Alex Stock.

NOTES ON SOURCES

1. Feret, Vol II, pp162–165.
2. *Ibid.*, pp168–174.
3. *The Times*, advertisement, 21 March, 1804.
4. Will proved 2 September 1657, PCC 338 Ruthven.
5. Ogilby's *Map of Middlesex* 1677, in which Munster House appears as 'Mustow'; Feret, Vol II, pp178 and 181.
6. *Ibid.*, pp181–196.
7. *Ibid.*, pp182–192.
8. Charles Feret found a card in a copy of Faulkner's *Historical and Topographical Account of Fulham* at Fulham Vicarage, which advertised the asylum.
9. Wilkie Collins, *Man and Wife* (1870), chapter 53.
10. Feret, Vol II, p204.
11. *Ibid.*, Vol III, pp6–8.
12. Molly Lefebure, *Murder with a Difference* (1958), pp56, 66.
13. Feret, Vol III, pp13–15.
14. Hasker, p1.
15. Feret, Vol III, p27.
16. *Ibid.*, Vol III, p31.
17. *Ibid.*, Vol III, pp42–43.
18. *Ibid.*, Vol III, pp56–59.

CHAPTER TEN
Villas at North End

'Whatever has happened to good old West Kensington?' sighed our landlady, whose basement flat in Normand Road had been our refuge during the flying bombs. Her over-genteel accent suited her nostalgic recollections of a very different neighbourhood to that in which she now found herself.

What had happened indeed? Where was the middle class respectability of yesteryear? Sadly scarred by bombing, many of its houses were empty and derelict; shops were boarded up and families had moved away. West Kensington was certainly not what it used to be and probably never would be so again. But what did 'it used to be'?

Its story is a comparatively brief one of little more than a century. In 1876 William Henry Gibbs and John P. Flew, jobbing builders from Dorset, who had already had some success in Kensington, decided to make another fortune on the 'wrong side of the tracks', west of the railway which ran along the bed of the old Counters Creek. The land was mainly occupied by market gardens, orchards and brickfields. They envisaged another South Kensington, but it never quite made the grade, for which they blamed the lack of a bridge across the railway into the heart of their new territory from Cromwell Road, though it might have taken more than that to fill the rows of huge, grey-brick, porch-fronted, balconied houses which were to line the roads on the estate owned by the descendants of the confectioner James Gunter.

Without such a bridge, the only routes to the West End were by Hammersmith or Lillie Road, and the new area could hardly be considered an extension of fashionable Kensington. Depression in the London housing market in the 1880s was affecting their sales. They had built over 1200 houses in North End,[1] which they had renamed West Kensington to link it with its prosperous neighbour, and many were still empty, in addition to vacant plots of land. Never lacking in enterprise, the partners decided that they would offer to build the bridge at their own expense. A Private Bill to promote the venture was passed by Parliament in 1884, despite opposition from the Metropolitan District Railway which feared competition from buses, but by now Gibbs and Flew were in such serious financial difficulty that they could not honour their offer. In 1885 the partnership was dissolved when their company, West Kensington Estate, which had a capital of a quarter of a million pounds, went into liquidation.[2] The campaign for the bridge, however, continued for another seventeen years with support from residents, the Vestry and, later, the borough council, but it was constantly opposed by vested interests. In the event the bridge, the West Cromwell Road, was not commenced until 1938 and it was opened in April 1942.

William Henry Gibbs was 33 when he set up business with John Flew at North End. Born in Portland, Dorset, his early years were spent there. He served an apprenticeship with a firm of Government engineers, constructing Weymouth breakwater, and later came to join their London office until he and Flew formed the partnership which endured for over a decade. Their first venture was to build a few houses on the Cedars estate, on what is now Auriol Road. From these small beginnings they developed to employing over seven hundred men at a time, sometimes touching a thousand, with their own brickfields, workshops and masonry yards. After West Kensington the partners moved on to Fulham proper, to large parts of the Munster Park and Salisbury area. They also built Munster Park Chapel, St Peter's Church, the Salisbury Hotel and Fulham Infirmary.

After Gibbs parted from Flew he set up on his own with considerable success before a setback made him bankrupt. However, it was not long before he recovered and was at work on new ventures in Hammersmith. John Flew, also operating independently, building blocks of flats in various parts of Fulham, met his crisis somewhat later, in 1904, but he too weathered the storm. Both men played a prominent part in local affairs and the Flew family continued both as developers, estate agents and landlords for several decades. The former partners died within three months of each other, in 1908.

Despite its early troubles, by the end of the Edwardian era their new development, West Kensington, had become popular with artists and literary figures, and it features in the works of authors like Compton Mackenzie and Ernest Raymond.

From the top floors of the new 'mansion flats' the highest building then on the horizon was the glass dome of the Empress Stadium (now replaced by the 22-storey Empress State Building of the Ministry of Defence), the last vestige of the old Earl's Court Exhibition, used mainly as an ice rink and for occasional boxing matches. The Congregational Church in Castletown Road boasted a square Norman tower, destroyed during the blitz and never replaced. In those days it was not difficult to believe that North End could once have been described by the historian Faulkner as having 'some very good houses on both sides of the road inhabited by several eminent and remarkable characters'.[3] A villa at North End was indeed a very acceptable address for wealthy businessmen as well as for the professional classes.

89. Programme for the Victorian Era Exhibition at Earl's Court in 1897.

The eastern portion of Lillie Road, which passes the end of North End Road market, is generally regarded as the boundary between Fulham proper and West Kensington. Lillie Road derives its name from the soldier-inventor, Sir John Scott Lillie, a veteran of the Peninsular Wars, who lived in the area in 1822. Not only did he invent the Lillie Rifle, an early form of machine gun, but also a method of road paving using gravel and wood blocks. He lived at the Hermitage, a large, rather ugly, three-storey house on the north-east corner of the junction of Lillie and North End Roads, with grounds of over 14 acres. A sale notice of 1815 described it as 'a delightful freehold villa with rich meadowlands, standing for two of three carriages, stabling for six horses, extensive gardens clothed with choicest fruit trees, a beautifully laid out sheet of water stocked with fish and three enclosures of very productive meadowland.'[4] The house itself was unusual in that every room had two doors, and some three, and it must also have been one of the very few Victorian villas to have its own indoor swimming pool, although this was probably installed much later in its history.

Earlier residents included Samuel Foote, an actor whose farces at the Haymarket Theatre drew large audiences in the late 18th century. The last occupants were the Somerset brewers, the Lovibonds. Henry Lovibond not only lived here but used part of the grounds on which to build the Cannon Brewery, formerly at Vauxhall and Chelsea. On his death he was succeeded by his son, Valentine, whose wife not only bore him five daughters, but also helped in the brewery management, studying chemistry and taking a full brewer's certificate.

The Hermitage and its remaining grounds were sold in 1897 and replaced by coal yards flanking the new railway.

Opposite the Hermitage, on the south-east corner of Lillie Road, was Cambridge Lodge, whose best known occupant was the engraver Francesco Bartolozzi, in the 1780s.

The Hermitage and Cambridge Lodge had both been built on the southern

90. The Big Wheel at Earl's Court.

91. *The bandstand at Earls Court.*

boundary of some open ground, owned by Fulham Rectory, known as Butts Close, so named for its use for archery. Adjoining this was a small field known as Nomans Land, a common medieval name for land awkward to divide up into strips for the manor tenants and just left vacant for occasional use.'Noemansland in ffulhamfield' is recorded in the Court Rolls in 1492, and the modern Normand Road is a corruption of the old name.

In 1649 Thomas Wyld of the Inner Temple purchased six acres of Butts Close together with Nomans Land. The main structure of Normand House dated from that time and the house remained in the Wyld family until the mid 1700s. In 1812 a Mr Jonas Hall and a Miss Pope opened an 'insane asylum for young ladies' there. The house remained an asylum for another sixty years, with some grisly stories of screams coming from the padded room over the coach house. Briefly it was used as a school after this, first as Princess Helena's School for Girls and then by Cardinal Manning as a school for pauper boys. The order of nuns of St Katharine bought the house in 1885 for work among first offender girls. The house, with its chapel added in 1899, was seriously damaged in the last war and eventually the site was cleared and Normand Park laid out.

On the western side of Normand Road, William Gibbs, now working separately from Flew, began in 1892 his most ambitious project, the construction of a huge estate of mansion flats. The area had been used as a brickfield by the firm of Crowle and Neeton and was now wasteland adjacent to the newly opened Queen's Club sports ground. What better name for the new development than Queen's Club Gardens? The *Fulham Chronicle* described the many amenities of the new estate in 1894, especially their 'perfect sanitary arrangements'.[5] Gibbs advertised kitchens fitted with 'kitcheners' (coal fire ovens with hot water boilers) and other refinements such as electric bells and Venetian blinds. To add to their classiness, the flats, built in over thirty blocks around central gardens and tennis courts, were named alphabetically after famous historical characters, from Matthew Arnold to the Palmyrian queen, Zenobia.

Gibbs was lucky to have the obligatory church already adjacent and so didn't have to build one. St Andrew's, the church whose tall spire overshadowed the northern side of the square, had been built nearly twenty years previously. It had risen from humble beginnings as a mission in 1868, and rebuilt as a proper church here in 1874. It was enlarged in 1895 during the

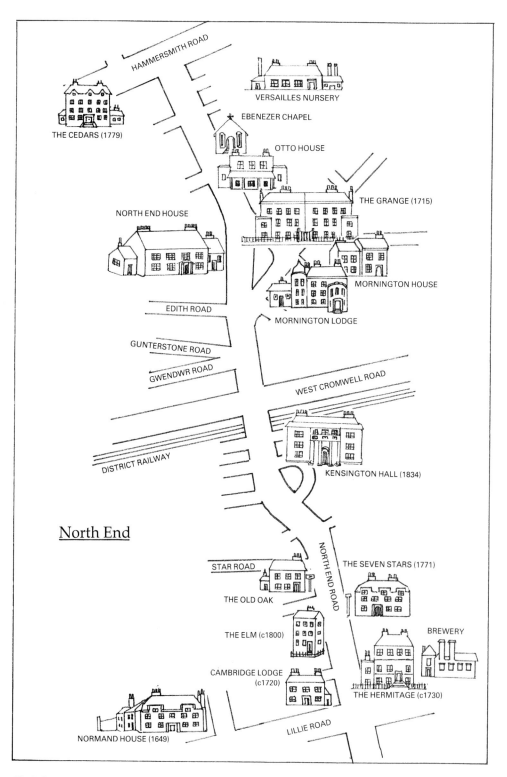

HAMMERSMITH ROAD

VERSAILLES NURSERY

EBENEZER CHAPEL

THE CEDARS (1779)

OTTO HOUSE

THE GRANGE (1715)

NORTH END HOUSE

MORNINGTON HOUSE

EDITH ROAD

MORNINGTON LODGE

GUNTERSTONE ROAD

GWENDWR ROAD

WEST CROMWELL ROAD

DISTRICT RAILWAY

KENSINGTON HALL (1834)

North End

NORTH END ROAD

STAR ROAD

THE SEVEN STARS (1771)

THE OLD OAK

THE ELM (c1800)

BREWERY

CAMBRIDGE LODGE
(c1720)

THE HERMITAGE (c1730)

NORMAND HOUSE (1649)

LILLIE ROAD

92. A sketch map of North End, showing many of the buildings mentioned.

93. *Tennis at Queens Club Gardens in 1910. Spencer to Owen Mansions are in the background.*

popular incumbency of the Anglo-Catholic vicar, the Rev Ernest Stafford Hilliard, and it was during his stay that the Church Lads Brigade was founded here. The church's more secular claim to fame is that the Church Lads football team formed the nucleus of Fulham Football Club. St Andrew's contains one of the oldest bells in London, still rung regularly for services. It came from the now demolished Wren church of St Martin Outwich in the City of London and is said to be the only London church bell to have survived the Great Fire; it was presented to St Andrew's by the Bishop of London at the time of the church's consecration.

The Queen's Club had been part of the Barons Court estate of another West Kensington landowner-developer, Sir William Palliser, who had intended to model this part of North End on neighbouring Earl's Court. His streets, set out in parallelograms, are named after his family associations in Ireland, such as Fairholme, Charleville and Comeragh. On his death, Gibbs and Flew bought part of his estate, which included ten acres laid out as a cricket ground. It was decided to promote this as a general sports club when the Princes Rackets and Tennis Club closed in 1887. The aim was to provide not only an athletic club for inter-Varsity contests, but a first class tennis club, and by 1900 there were not only thirty grass tennis courts surrounded by a running track, but indoor courts, rackets courts, a cricket pitch and an asphalt rink which could be flooded in winter for skating. Today it is the venue for many top tournaments and the Lawn Tennis Association headquarters are situated here.

The Metropolitan and District Railway's extension to Hammersmith in the 1870s drove a barrier through the new neighbourhood. At Baron's Court Gibbs and Flew solved the problem by bridging the line at Gliddon Road, which was crowned by Baron's Court Station in 1905.

A social, rather than a physical, division existed between those who lived north of St Andrew's and their servants and tradesmen to the south, as jobbing builders got busy on rows of smaller terraced houses in May Street, Turneville, Archel, Chesson and Bramber Roads and other new streets created between North End and Normand Roads. Their many inhabitants, for most were in multi-occupation, were at least well-served with hostelries – no less than five in the space of a hundred yards or so between the junctions of Lillie Road and

94. Old tenements at Gibbs Green, 1895.

May Street. The Elm, on the corner of Archel Road, had been a beer shop for some years before being rebuilt in 1899. Opposite, the Seven Stars is mentioned in the parish books in 1771, although rebuilt after the 2nd World War. Beside this pub was the garden entrance to the Earl's Court Exhibition, the grounds of which extended as far as the railway on the north, its Great Wheel, 300 feet high, towering behind the houses in old photographs. Although the popularity of the grounds faded after the Victorian era, they survived until 1914, but by 1920 the site was derelict and hidden by hoardings. The Old Oak on the corner of Star Road also began its life as a beer shop before several rebuildings, but the Clarence, built in 1864 as a typical Victorian 'hotel', was enlarged in 1894.

In contrast to this proliferation of drinking places was the Bethel Chapel of the New Methodist Connexion, a group of whose devotees moved from a chapel in Radnor Street, Chelsea in the 1860s to a temporary 'iron' (corrugated) hall on the corner of Chesson Road in the 1860s, followed by a permanent chapel in 1887, designed by the architect A.H. Goodall in a style known as Geometric Decorated. Closed before the war, it is now a Bedding Centre.

Despite his associations with the area William Gibbs had no connection with Gibbs Green, the small portion of North End Road where it takes a sharp bend to the left just past Star Road. The ancient name is recorded in Court Rolls as early as 1428. Its past history includes a market garden famed for the excellence of its tomatoes, followed for nine years (1870–79) by the Star Running Grounds. On the North End Road frontage in Victorian times was a dairy, Pearson's, where the milk was brought in daily from the owner's farm at Heston, and nearby an early 'Round House' fire station. The West Ken Super Kinema, opened in 1922, closed during the war and had become a removal depot before demolition in the 1960s.

The earliest surviving buildings on the Butts Close land is the row of small cottages built in 1848, now a modernised terrace called Lanfrey Place. It was formerly named Ebenezer Place, commemorating the Sunday School there run by a devout Baptist.

In the 1880s, members of the Congregational chapel in Allen Street, Kensington, raised £18,000 to build a new church to serve the growing population of West Kensington at Castletown Road. It is now the Bhavan Centre of

Indian Culture, opened in the 1970s by Prime Minister James Callaghan.

West Kensington Station, opened in 1877 as 'North End', was built on the site of King's Cottage, next door to the ancient hostlery, the Three Kings, established in 1750.

Although technically in Hammersmith, being to the north of the Parrs Ditch which ran through the playing fields, the demolition of St Paul's School's handsome 'St Pancras Gothic' building in the 1960s, when the school moved to Barnes, was lamented in Fulham. The ultimate development of the site became the subject of a long, bitter and unsuccessful campaign. A comparatively modern building (of the the 1870s), the school's design was not always popular. In 1893 Percy Fitzgerald wrote in his *London City Suburbs* that he considered it a 'vast dull red pile'[6] but its expanse of playing fields, open to the public as spectators of rugger and cricket matches, provided a welcome open space, now lost in the dense development of the West London College and flats.

The curved line of Talgarth Road follows an old path first known as Warner's and later Deadman's Lane – the latter name from a family who ran a market garden here rather than from a more sinister origin. Between Deadman's Lane and Hammersmith Road was Washes Farm. This was once owned by William Earsby, who bequeathed three pieces of land, the rents of which were to buy Hampshire Kersey (a coarse woollen cloth) to make 'petticoats and waistcoats with good binding and clasps', for 'six poor widows on Fulham side of good repute and quiet conversation – to be continued six one year and six the next until the world's end.' Another benefactor to the area was Richard Hunt, who lived at a large, rambling house called The Cedars, and who built a chapel to St Mary which was consecrated in 1813. This building, brick with a central

95. St Paul's School.

96. The Grange, c1900.

97. Miss Esther Lawrence, first headmistress of the Froebel Demonstration School, 1892, and later principal of the Froebel Educational Institute.

spire, was bombed in the last war and replaced by a new church in the 1960s.

After Hunt's death in 1818 The Cedars became a girls' school; this was demolished in 1882 and nos. 129–135 Hammersmith Road stand on its site.

In that part of Talgarth Road, known as Colet Gardens, the Froebel Educational Institute was founded in the 1890s to pursue the kindergarten teaching methods pioneered by the German educationalist, Friedrich Froebel (1782–1852). Run by Marie Michaelis, it began as a training college for women teachers in 1894, and two years later a model school and kindergarten were added. The college moved out to Roehampton at the end of the 1st World War, and was joined by the School in 1946. The building is now occupied by the Royal Ballet School.

The best-known of the North End villas was The Grange – it was also the most enduring, surviving until the 1950s when, despite protests, it was demolished. Situated at the point of North End 'Lane' where it took a sharp turn northwest towards Hammersmith Road, its site is now occupied by Council flats of the same name. It began as two cottages; these were demolished c1715 and a double-fronted villa built on their site. The Grange, quite often divided into two residences, has had two famous occupants. The novelist, Samuel Richardson, was here for fifteen years from 1738. (Richardson's *Pamela* is regarded as being the first modern novel.) Then, in 1867, the Pre-Raphaelite artist, Edward Burne-Jones, took the house. A visitor to The Grange during his tenancy was the young Rudyard Kipling, whose aunt, Georgiana, was Burne-Jones' wife. Christmas and holidays spent here were the few happy periods in the young Kipling's life after he was separated from his parents in India, to be educated in England.

In the garden of The Grange was a grotto embellished with shells and star shapes and curious fossils. This seems to have disappeared in later years

98. *The studio of Sir Edward Burne-Jones at The Grange, c1898.*

although compensation came from the house's last residents, the Crowther family, of antique masonry fame, who displayed monuments, statues and other picturesque stone work there. There was also an ancient mulberry tree, a huge walnut and a briar rose which Burne-Jones, who worked in a garden studio, immortalised in his picture of *The Sleeping Beauty*.

Other villas on the Gunter estate included North End House (now the site of flats built in the 1930s bearing the same name), which had grounds of 6½ acres that contained a lake. The most interesting occupant was James Wild, a collector of books, furniture and curiosities.

Another villa of the same name was built in North End Lane in the early years of the 19th century by Thomas Slator, founder of a Kensington firm of butchers. Slator had another house at North End, Kensington Hall, a sombre pile described as a 'heavy brick building with an ornamented cement elevation relieved by fluted columns.'[7] Erected in 1834, it stood empty so long it became known as Slator's Folly. It was later used as a Roman Catholic orphanage and once that had gone it was demolished, although its name is perpetuated by the flats, Kensington Hall Gardens.

Another of North End's desirable residences was Mornington Lodge, the home for a time of William Gibbs. This stood on the corner of the present Mornington Avenue, on a site now occupied by Council flats. Mornington House, just to the north, is said to have been built as a shooting box for the third Earl of Mornington, elder brother of the Duke of Wellington. Somewhere in somebody's back garden around the end of Matheson Road, there may still be some of the stones said to have been taken from Alexander Pope's home at Twickenham.

Fitzjames Avenue, built in 1900, were the grandest of all West Kensington's mansion flats. They were provided with lifts and most of the apartments

99. *Rudyard Kipling. Oil painting by Sir Philip Burne-Jones.*

had separate servants' quarters. Nevertheless, they rubbed shoulders with the shabbier Vernon, Southcombe (previously Devonshire) and Munden Streets built in the mid 19th century on land belonging to the Vernon Investment Association, which was formed in 1846 by Bloomsbury tradesmen who met at the Vernon Arms, in Southampton Street, Pentonville. Southcombe Street recalls a sad incident in 1814 when John Southcombe, a visitor from Devon, was killed by the Bath Mail Coach here.

The Police Court in Southcombe Street, built in 1856, replaced a ramshackle old building in Brook Green known as the Twenty Steps, from its approach up a flight of wooden stairs. Dorcas Terrace, on the Hammersmith Road frontage, is even older, dating from 1824 and is named for the wife of its builder, a man called Payne. The future of this terrace has been in the melting pot for nearly two decades.

Counters Bridge (now Addison Bridge) carried the old Roman road over Counters Creek. Its maintenance was the responsibility of the lord of the manor of Fulham, in this case the Bishop of London, and orders for its repair appear frequently in the court rolls. Three acres on the Fulham side of the creek were bought in the 17th century by the trustees of the Bishop King charities, which supplied the poor with beef and bread. This land was leased for building to a William Vale early in the 19th century and his developments included the houses which still stand in Addison Bridge Place next to the present Hand and Flower, but otherwise his buildings in the area were of a mean nature.

West Kensington suffered much during the last war. Landmines caused widespread damage in the area around Gwendwr Road (the small park Gwendwr Gardens, is a memorial to those who died). The West Kensington of between-the-wars died with them. Gone was Dawson's, the drapers, Rapson's, the old-fashioned grocers. Gone too the toy shops, Marchmont's and Peckover's. Today's West Kensington is dominated by the auxiliaries of bed-sitter land, fast food restaurants. Families tend to be in the Council flats and the young, single people are in the houses now, almost without exception, divided into flats.

The Talgarth Road section of the A4 has retained its Gibbs and Flew terrace of grey-brick houses on the southern side, but they are now unhappily sandwiched between heavy road traffic in front and railway lines behind. The link with Kensington over the railway, which was the dream of those Victorian builders, has been West Kensington's downfall instead of its salvation. Without it this north end of Fulham might have retained more of the characteristics of a pleasant residential area which its builders envisaged. It is not, in other words, 'what it used to be'.

NOTES ON SOURCES

1   Hasker, pp109–111.
2   *Ibid.*, p126; Feret, Vol II, p278.
3   Faulkner, p329.
4   Feret, Vol II, p271.
5   *Fulham Chronicle*, 29 Dec 1893 and 19 Jan 1894, and advertisement 11 May 1900.
6   P. Fitzgerald, *London City Suburbs* (1893), p74.
7   Feret, Vol II, p285.

CHAPTER ELEVEN

Many Mansions

'It is the prettiest baby house in the world, a pavilion rather than a villa, all green paint white chintz and looking glass...' – thus the description by Benjamin Disraeli, of a riverside home, called Rosebank, not far from Craven Cottage. Sadly, it is no more. It has gone, together with all the other mansions of Fulham's past, except Hurlingham House.

Rosebank was one of the smallest of Fulham's grander houses, but it was certainly one of the most lovely. The estate on which it was built was leased by Lord Cholmondley, Lord Steward of the Royal Household, in 1809, and, inspired by a Swiss chalet he had seen, he built Rosebank using timber from his estates. His successors, Lord and Lady Londonderry, gave lavish parties here in the gardens by the river.[1] After being destroyed by fire in 1864 and rebuilt, the house was finally demolished in 1896 and the grounds developed.

Where the Distillery now stands, on the Hammersmith borders of Fulham's riverside, stood Brandenburgh House, one of the most impressive and interesting houses in London. It was built for Sir Nicholas Crispe, a trader in goods and slaves between Africa and the West Indies, who was granted, with five others, exclusive right to trade with Guinea from 1632. In 1637 Crispe's company complained that 'interlopers were infringing its monopoly by transporting nyggers to the West Indies'. He was, however, attacked as a monopolist during his service as a Member for Winchelsea in the Long Parliament, and ordered to attend a Committee of Grievance to 'submit his patents for the sole trade with Guinea for the import of red wood and making and vending beads.' He was expelled from the House, but he was wealthy enough to develop his estate of 86 acres in Fulham, particularly his new house situated 'in sweet and wholesome air, built very lofty, regular and magnificent after the modern manner, of brick, cornered with stone with a handsome cupola at top'.[2] Crispe supported the King during the Civil War and as a result had his property sequestered. General Fairfax took up quarters at his house in Fulham where Lady Crispe was still living, and in 1647 there is a report that a man posing as a French cook tried to poison the Parliamentary visitors by serving up what he called a 'French Quickshas'.[3] Crispe recovered his estates after the Restoration, but died in 1666. He ordered that there should be little pomp at his funeral and that his heart should be 'embalmed and be put in a small black urn made of hardest stone and fastened in it, placed on a pillar of the best and hardest black marble to be set up in Hammersmith chapel near my pew'.[4] (This chapel-of-ease has since been replaced by St Paul's, Hammersmith.) Faulkner, in his *History of Hammersmith*, said that 'It was the custom to take out the heart on the anniversary of its interment and to refresh it with a glass of wine. At length, after the expiration of more than a century and half, it became decayed and was finally enclosed in a leaden case'. Oddly enough, the rest of his body had been interred in the churchyard of St Mildred's, Bread Street, in the City of London, and when that was cleared in 1898 his remains were brought back to Hammersmith and reunited with those of his heart.

Prince Rupert, nephew of Charles I, bought Crispe's Fulham house in 1683 and gave it to his mistress, Margaret Hughes, an actress. She lived here for ten years, during which time she gave birth to a daughter called Ruperta, a name which left little doubt as to the parentage.

100. Brandenburgh House, c1810.

In 1748 the house was bought by George Bubb Dodington (later Lord Melcombe), a changecoat politician known as 'Sillybubb' by the satirists.'Silly-bubb' was not an apt name for him. An opportunist he may have been, but he was certainly no fool. A man of wit and culture, and a scholar, he was respected by literary men of his day. Dodington renamed the house 'Le Trappe' after the famous monastery in France, and he spent a fortune modernising it and adding a magnificent gallery to its salon. At the front his family crest was laid out in pebbles in the turf. He surrounded himself at Le Trappe with friends who resembled the characters of a Restoration comedy. Described as 'a mis-anthrope, a courtier and a quack', they were Thomas Wyndham, whom he made his heir, who had 'the sullenness of a grumblestone', Dr Thompson an 'out of practice physician' and 'a more dirty animal was never seen on the outside of a pigsty', and Sir William Breton, Privy Purse to the King 'with the vanity and self conceit of an antiquated coxcomb.'[5]

A Mrs Sturt inherited the house on Wyndham's death. She used it for the production of society theatricals and masquerades.[6] In 1792 the Margrave of Brandenburgh, Anspach and Bayreuth bought the house. His wife, the former Lady Craven, was also keen on theatricals, and so was built here a small Gothic theatre by the river so that she could indulge her interest and be diverted in 'charming contrast to accounts, bills and changes of domestics and chamber-lains and other things quite odious to me'. In her memoirs she noted that 'We had at Brandenburgh House thirty servants in livery with grooms and a stud of sixty horses. Our expenses were enormous although I curtailed them with every possible economy.' There were five state apartments with walls lined with white satin. In addition there was a ballroom, a magnificent library, a

101. Craven Cottage, c1820.

private chapel and the gardens were laid out with rare and expensive trees.

The house's most illustrious days were yet to come. In 1820 it was taken by Caroline of Brunswick, consort of the Prince Regent (the later George IV). She was a plain and eccentric woman and the marriage was not a happy one; they had one child, the ill-fated Princess Charlotte, who died in childbirth after her own marriage to Leopold of Saxe Coburg. Caroline's conduct caused more and more scandal (no less than her husband's, but more was expected of her) and the Prince Regent insisted on a Parliamentary enquiry into her behaviour. In the ensuing years of recriminations and bitterness both of these two unattractive people had their enthusiastic supporters. For example, the Thames watermen and lightermen sailed up the river to the lawns in front of Brandenburgh House, and workmen marched there with banners, to present her with loyal addresses.[7] Similar deputations came from other quarters, and after she had died at Brandenburgh House, her funeral was the scene of tremendous public demonstrations.

Her death also marked the end of Brandenburgh House. The fixtures of the house, such as fireplaces, columns and floors, were sold and eventually the building was razed.[8]

Craven Cottage was not nearly so grand, but it was very pretty, rather like the famous Queen's Cottage in the bluebell woods at Kew Gardens, with a thatched roof and dormer windows. Lady Craven lived here during her estrangement from her husband and before her remarriage to the Margrave of Brandenburgh. A subsequent owner was Charles King, a well-known money lender, who gave extravagant parties here. He was known to have a detailed knowledge of the peerage and their fortunes.'By dint of sundry kind attentions to the clerks of the leading banking houses he was aware of the balances they kept and the credit attached to their names'.[9] By now, Craven Cottage was embellished with an unsuitable colonnade, and the interior had been decorated in Egyptian style.

Lord George Bulwer Lytton took Craven Cottage for a time. It was here that he wrote *The Last of the Barons*, and entertained Louis Napoleon (later Napoleon III), who described the place as 'the most beautiful villa'. The house's final owner was an American, Walter Bentley Woodbury, who had the idea of turning the grounds into pleasure gardens, but nothing came of it. Craven Cottage was destroyed by fire in 1888 and in 1896 the young Fulham Football Club bought the site of the house and grounds for its football pitch.

As Wimbledon line trains leave Putney Bridge Station to rumble over the iron bridge across the river, they pass just east of where Willow Bank, an elegant riverside house, stood.[10] It had terraced gardens extending to three acres by the river, land used in much earlier times by osier dealers. By the mid–18th century a house was here, built by a City banker, Sir Francis Gosling, Master of the Stationers' Company, whose banking house was eventually absorbed into Barclays Bank. One of George III's doctors, Francis Milman, President of the Royal College of Physicians, lived here for thirteen years from 1791 and left it, according to Faulkner, in 'an unoccupied and ruinous condition'. Its successor, Willow Bank, was built on piles. Among its residents were two remarkable men, a Mr Delafield, the son of a wealthy brewer, who had sold out his shareholding in the business, and 'Captain Webster', a theatrical manager. Willow Bank was a popular society venue, where lavish entertainments and charity garden parties were common. This life-style came to a rude end when rumours circulated that the pair were living beyond their income, and they made off to Brussels, never to be seen again. The sale of the contents of Willow Bank lasted for ten days.

One of the last occupants was Frederick Swindell, who had risen from the job as a 'boots' in a Nottingham hotel to become wealthy and an owner of race horses. He was not at Willow Bank long because soon after his arrival the Thames flooded the house. 'This has settled me', he remarked to a friend, 'I can stand a good many things but I cannot stand being washed out of my own house!' In 1889 Willow Bank was bought by the District Railway Company and demolished.

East of Willow Bank, between the river and Hurlingham Road, was Ranelagh House, demolished in 1892 to make way for an estate which now includes Ranelagh Gardens. Between 1764 and 1775, Philip Stephens, another self-made man, acquired over 55 acres of land in this part of Fulham. His heiress married the sixth Viscount Ranelagh, who was cantankerous enough to object to picnic parties on the river, especially if they were bold enough to get out of their boats and eat their lunch on his shore. On one occasion he was so incensed that he pushed their boats into the river, smashed the oars and kicked the party out of his front gates. The boating party sued for assault and in court their lawyer made a vigorous attack on the Viscount's character. Ranelagh retaliated by going to the lawyer's chambers and horse-whipping him. A further law suit ensued but was never resolved since Ranelagh died in 1820.

The estate descended to his eldest son, who was only eight years old and still at school. The 7th Viscount spent a number of years in the Army and when he did return to Fulham, he lived in his father's adjoining property, Mulgrave House. Ranelagh House itself had been let to a succession of tenants, the last of whom was Reginald Herbert, who established a country club, the Ranelagh Club, there until the lease was finally closed in 1884 and it moved to Barn Elms across the river at Barnes.

Mulgrave and Little Mulgrave House stood east of Ranelagh House, on the estate. The latter was a simple three-storey Georgian villa which Fèret

102. Mulgrave House, c1895.

described as having 'narrow passages and staircases, oddly contrived cupboards and quaint recesses which seem to remind one of days when secret chambers were necessary adjuncts of a mansion.' The name 'Mulgrave' was taken from its tenant in the first years of the 19th century, Henry Phipps, the third Baron Mulgrave. The building was demolished in 1894.

Mulgrave House was taken in 1844 by a Mr Price, alias Charles Louis de Bourbon, Duke of Normandy and Pretender to the French throne. There were three attempts on his life, the third at Mulgrave House. The *Illustrated London News* of 4 January 1845 reported that: 'The self-styled Duke of Normandy who now occupies Mulgrave House, Fulham, where he has been for some time carrying out his invention of explosive materials to be employed in warfare, was again shot at on Thursday evening by some unknown assassin.'

After Lord Ranelagh's tenancy – he paid £100 a year rental – the Ecclesiastical Commissioners leased Mulgrave House to the Hurlingham Club, together with its 15 acres, including the lake which still forms an important feature of the beautiful grounds. Hurlingham House, which is now central to the Hurlingham Club, was built in 1760 by Dr William Cadogan on nine acres of land leased from the Bishop. Cadogan, already a Fulham resident, specialised in children's diseases, although he also published a *Dissertation on the Gout and all Chronic Diseases* which became a popular medical textbook. Hurlingham House was sold after his death to a relative who added the wings on either side of the central portion with a pillared neo-Classical frontage. He did not keep it long and it passed on to several wealthy residents, one of whom added a further 16 acres to the grounds.

The origins of the elite Hurlingham Club were humble. Frank Heathcote,

who became the tenant in 1867, founded the Hurlingham Club to pursue the sport of pigeon-shooting. In those days pigeons were released from traps and extensive gambling went on as to the number which could then be shot. Members had to pay £2.4s for a dozen blue rocks (the common London pigeon), but it was the wagers that could be expensive – one member in 1882 lost £160 in a day.

Gradually, polo was introduced from India, where it was popular with the colonial administrators, in particular with the military. The first polo match at Hurlingham was in June 1874, between teams from the Royal Horse Guards and the Monmouthshire Polo Club; the spectators included the Prince and Princess of Wales. The sport's social status continued to climb and in 1887, when a gala match was played to celebrate the Jubilee of Queen Victoria, no less than thirty royals were present. But polo is an expensive sport and by 1886 Hurlingham was having to provide boxes for 27 ponies, stabling for 45 carriage horses and there was always the problem of getting members to actually pay the forage bills they ran up.

One of Fulham's most elderly residents, Mrs Beatrice Roberts, then aged 91, recalled the excitement of polo matches at Hurlingham in Edwardian days. There were lines of carriages down Broomhouse Lane and she and her friends would peer through gaps in the fence to catch a glimpse of the women in their vast befeathered and flowered hats, and the men in their formal attire. Occasionally the gatekeeper would let them in the side entrance to watch if they were quiet.

Originally the club grounds stretched from the river to Hurlingham Road, and from Broomhouse Lane to the east and Mulgrave House to the west. When the latter was acquired a new polo ground was installed on a site now occupied

103. Hurlingham Club ponies, c1905.

104. Women's archery at Hurlingham, 1895. From the Illustrated London News.

105. Hurlingham House, c1867.

by the Council flats, Sulivan Court, on the opposite side of Broomhouse Lane. In time, the Club doubled its landholding.

Pigeon-shooting went altogether – it was, in fact, banned by Parliament in 1905 as being cruel. But the Club had already added other sports to its activities. They included tennis, croquet, archery and golf. The All England Croquet Club established itself at Hurlingham and it is interesting that the sport is now enjoying a revival as a serious, rather than a social, sport at the same venue. Lawn tennis, popular in England from the 1870s, was not played at Hurlingham until the 1880s, when racquets were kept for hire at 2s 6d a time. Golf was played on a nine hole course which extended on to part of the polo ground. More dramaticallly, the Royal Aero Club organised five balloon contests here up to 1912. It was also a venue for early motor rallies.

In 1928 Hurlingham was seriously affected by the great Thames flood and during the 2nd World War the no. 1 polo ground was dug up for allotments.

As the sports and the attendances increased in the 1930s, so did the enthusiasm of Fulham Council for buying the site for housing. It was not until after the last war that much of the area was acquired to create Hurlingham Park and sports arena and Council housing, leaving the Club only its house, river frontage, tennis courts and croquet lawns. More details of the life and times of the Hurlingham Club may be found in the book by Captain Taprell Dorning ('Taffrail'), published in 1953.[11]

In the south-east corner of Bishops Park once stood a house so ornate and so large that many newcomers imagined it was the Palace itself. Called Pryors Bank, it was built soon after 1837 by two antiquaries, Thomas Baylis and William Letchmore Whitmore, in an antique style, with battlements, turretted chimneys and 23 rooms. It was filled throughout with curiosities. In *A Walk from London to Fulham*, Thomas Croker says 'Mr Baylis gleaned a rich harvest from the number of brokers shops and saved from oblivion articles of various periods that were daily in the course of macadamisation or being consumed for firewood'.[12] When they sold the house in 1841, the auctioneer advertised that 'an enormous expense has been encountered and consummate taste exercised to effect so perfect an achievement…' The grounds were 'laid out in imitation of Dropmore, grottos, arbours and fountains diversify the scene and a terrace walk extending 250 feet along the Thames affords an opportunity of enjoying the passing scenery of the river…' Another antiquary occupied it for the next thirty years and it was demolished in 1897, being replaced by a mock-Tudor villa used first as a restaurant pavilion and now as offices of the Borough's Parks and Cemeteries department.

Just west of the old bridge (its site now taken by the line of the present crossing) was Egmont Villa, the home of the Georgian writer and satirist, Theodore Hook, from 1831–41. Hook was unfortunate enough, when he was a civil servant, to be wrongly accused of embezzlement and although eventually cleared of criminal responsibility, he did have his estates confiscated and was himself imprisoned in the Sponging House at Shire Lane, a debtors' prison, and in the King's Bench Prison. It was during his incarceration that he returned to his earlier literary leanings and began to write novels. Despite the popularity of his books he lived beyond his income and died poor at Egmont Villa, leaving a widow and five children; he was buried in Fulham churchyard.

106. Theodore Hook.

Lonsdale House (later Carnworth House), the most easterly of the riverside homes, was, during the residence of Sir John and Lady Shelley in the mid Victorian era, the scene of some splendid social occasions known as Strawberry Teas on Saturday afternoons in June and July, at one of which Mr Gladstone is said to have proposed to his wife-to-be.

Broom House, on the western corner of Broomhouse Lane, was described by Feret as 'perhaps the most elegant mansion to be found in Fulham'.[13] Built facing the river in nine acres of grounds, it was generally occupied in the 19th century by members of the British Raj, including Laurence Sulivan, whose grandfather had been chairman of the East India Company. He married Elizabeth Temple, younger sister of Lord Palmerston, and the Prime Minister was a frequent visitor here. She died when she was 47 and her husband founded the Elizabethan School in Broomhouse Lane in her memory. The house survived until the death of his daughter, Charlotte, in 1911, when it and its grounds were absorbed by the Hurlingham Club.

Under the auctioneer's hammer in 1829 was Cole Hill House, at the southern end of Fulham Palace Road. It was built in 1770 by James Madden, the son of a West Indies merchant, in Italian style, and designed by Henry Holland, architect of the Theatre Royal at Drury Lane and the original Brighton Pavilion. Madden, who lived here for forty years, had fifteen children, the youngest of whom, Sir George Allan Madden, kept a diary of life in this part of Fulham and his friendship with the Margrave of Brandenburgh and his wife. After the house was auctioned its 'beautiful pleasure grounds' were embellished by Joseph Paxton. The last owner was James English, a manufacturer of playing cards, and the house was demolished in 1890; small terraces mark its site.

Fulham's vanished mansions are its sadness. Few were of any great architectural merit, their associations being of greater interest than their appearance, but in hindsight, their gardens alone would have provided beautiful parks in an area which possesses so little attractive open space and the riverside estates, if preserved, would have rivalled any reach of the upper Thames.

NOTES ON SOURCES

1 Feret, Vol III, pp87–9.
2 Bowack, Vol II, pp36, 37.
3 *Perfect Occurrences*, 10 Sept 1647, Vol II, p250.
4 Last Will and Testament of Sir Nicholas Crispe, 23 February 1665, PCC 42 Mico.
5 *The Memoirs of Richard Cumberland, son of the Rev Denison Cumberland, Vicar of Fulham*.
6 *Life and Letters of Sir Gilbert Elliot, first Earl of Minto*. Letter from Sir Gilbert to his wife, 13 June 1789. See Feret, Vol III, p74.
7 *John Bull*, 29 January, 1821.
8 Most of Queen Caroline's furniture, plate, pictures books etc, were removed from Brandenburgh House on her death and taken to her town residence, Cambridge House, South Audley Street, where the effects were sold by Mr G. Robins on 20–26 February 1822. Another sale, of furniture, pictures and books, took place on 9 February 1822 at Brandenburgh House, an event which encouraged speculation in *John Bull* on 17 February 1822.
9 Captain Rees Howell Gronow, *Reminiscences and Recollections*, p132.
10 Feret, Vol III, pp231–233.
11 Captain Taprell Dorning ('Taffrail'), *The Hurlingham Club, 1869–1953* (Hurlingham Club, 1953).
12 *Fraser's Magazine*, December 1845; 'Ancient Domestic Furniture', *Gentleman's Magazine*, January 1842.
13 Feret, Vol III, p246.

CHAPTER TWELVE

Church and Churchmen

A shortage of funds in 1870 prevented Fulham from building a new parish church.[1] Sir George Gilbert Scott had been commissioned to design a more commodious building, which would have been entirely different from the old, but in the event the parish couldn't afford it. Ten years later, Arthur Blomfield, architect son of the Bishop of London, designed instead the present building which retains the ancient tower and features the Kentish ragstone and battlements of the old building. It was a fortuitous delay, for Blomfield's building suits its setting better.

The first reference to a church in Fulham is in 1154, contained in records of a tithe dispute. During rebuilding work in 1880 the remains of the foundations were uncovered, including a stone attached to the shafting of a window jamb of *c*1150.

Blomfield's church is much larger than its predecessor and, because of the frequent flooding of the Thames, the floor is three feet higher. The old tower is 96 feet high and described by Samuel Knight, the architect who restored it in 1908, as the finest medieval steeple in London excepting that of Southwark Cathedral.[2] Work on it probably began in the 14th century but it was still going on in 1440. That year the people of Fulham petitioned the king that stone for the church and the workmen employed on it, should not be taken away for the 'king's own project' (the building of Eton College).

Numerous pictures exist of the old church, the earlier ones depicting the little wooden spire which surmounted the tower, known to locals as the 'pepper-pot', which was removed in 1845. Feret described the old building as an irregular barn-like structure with a low red-tiled roof, and Walford's *Old and New London* dismisses it as 'little else than a collection of high pews and deep galleries contained within four walls pierced at intervals with holes for the admission of light – in fact one of the worst specimens of suburban churches which have of late years so rapidly and happily disappeared before the growing taste for a purer and more devotional style of church architecture.' There was a nave and two aisles, no chancel, but merely a recess for the communion table, and the vaulted semi-circular roof was lit with attic windows 'made of wood coloured blue'; a deep, broad gallery, supported by wooden pillars, extended along the north and south sides and across the western end. In the galleries, seats were reserved for the pupils of the National Schools. Special pews were provided for the Bishop, his family and household, and in the north-west corner was a large square pew for the Limpany family next to their large family monument. Most pews were privately rented and quite often the subject of disputes. In 1588 an incident occurred in which a 'mad blade called Maddocks' who had married a gentleman's daughter in Fulham, decided to assert his right to a pew.'Upon Easter Day he came in a warlike manner with rapier and target to the church when the Bishop and all his men were at the Court and there thrust in his mother and his sister into the Bishop's wife's seat and troubled his daughters being come to Communion'.[3]

Beneath the tower was a small chapel which is now part of the church. From it spiral steps lead up to the ringing chamber below the belfry. The sound of the Fulham bells carried on the west wind is one of the lingering delights of a

former age; noted for their sweetness of tone, the bells have been compared to those of Magdalen College, Oxford, and are pitched in the same key of E as those of Exeter Cathedral. They are first mentioned in an inventory of 1549, and again during the Civil War when they were 'overthrown by soldiers'. They were recast soon after, and again in 1728 when, in their transportation by river to Fulham, the barge sank. When the bells were retrieved and hung in the tower, crowds gathered on the banks of Fulham and Putney to listen to the trial ringing. The bells were rung, as everywhere else, more frequently in those days – at religious festivals, on birthdays of members of the royal family, and at times of national celebration.[4] Funeral knells for parishioners were charged at half a crown, and the bell was also rung at 5am and 8pm to tell villagers the time of day. Records of special ringings are kept in the bell chamber and number over 230 in 250 years. In 1735 the Society of Fulham Youths rang a complete peal of 10,080 bob majors in 6 hours and 40 minutes.

A church clock, with one face, is first mentioned in 1637, when a man was paid six shillings a year for winding it. That which appears on illustrations of the old church was bought in 1689, and it lasted until 1883 when the church was presented with a new one, paid for by private subscription, and which strikes the Cambridge quarters on the bells.

A 1549 Inventory, conducted by Royal Commissioners, gives a detailed account of the church furnishings before and after the Reformation. The object of the exercise was not only to purge the churches and chapels of 'Popish' ornaments and trappings but also to keep track of them so that they did not fall

107. All Saints church, 1817. Drawing by I. Hassell.

into private hands. It was alleged that 'Privatemen's halls were hung with altar cloths, their beds and tables covered with copes and chalices used as drinking cups at meals.' The Fulham Inventory listed those items disposed of, which included practically all the vestments, described variously as made of russet or green satin from Bruges, red velvet, green damask etc, all of which were sold to a merchant tailor and a girdler in Wood Street, in the City, presumably for recycling in other garments. Several crosses, candlesticks, bells and vessels were disposed of but the church was allowed to keep two chalices, a silver gilt pyx, three white copes, altar cloths and some linen.[5] An inventory in 1670, ten years after the Restoration, shows that the church's wordly goods had been reduced to some plate, nine leather chairs, some of which were broken, and 'six very old cushions of green baize unfit to use'.

The present church plate, rarely displayed nowadays, includes two large silver flagons, made in Nuremburg, presented in 1663 by a Mrs Katherine Hues, a silver paten presented in 1684, a 17th-century silver gilt chalice decorated with garnets, and the silver head of a beadle's staff, surmounted by a man holding a stick, inscribed with the names of its donors.

A great benefactor in the early 17th century was Dr Thomas Edwardes, Chancellor to Bishop John King, a very wealthy man, who left bequests to his family totalling over £10,000[6] and a small sum to establish a schoolroom and vestry over the north porch. In March 1722 it was said that this Vestry Room was 'in a very ruinous condition and unfit for use and so damp that it spoils the books and everything else in it.' Not only this, but 'our Vicar Dr Dwight [son of the Fulham potter] being very lame and much out of order in his health cannot go upstairs into the old room where the inhabitants sometimes meet to do the business of the parish.' This room was taken down sixty years later.

A little of the old glass survived the 19th century rebuilding. It included that now in the north porch which bears the arms of the Carthusian priory of Jesus of Bethlehem at Sheen[7] – the priors derived income from Fulham church after they were granted the Rectory in 1420. Faulkner, noting the old church, said that the 'curious Gothic windows on the south aisle were destroyed in the great repair in 1770...those ignorant contractors chose rather to put in new wooden frames than to endeavour to restore the antique stonework which might however have been easily effected, only one window escaped the hands of the barbarians'.

The present glass includes the east window memorial erected by Arthur Blomfield in memory of his father, the Bishop, one for Bishop Archibald Tait, who laid the foundation stone of the new church, and a third for Bishop Jackson who consecrated it. The Children's Window next to the north door was paid for by children of the parish; it depicts Christ blessing the children, one of whom is the likeness of one of the then Vicar's children. The west window below the tower, rebuilt in 1840, was shattered in the last war but fortunately the shields had already been removed for safety.[8]

The font, which now stands near the north door, was presented to the old church in 1622 by churchwarden Thomas Hill and bears an inscription to that effect. The most exciting discovery made in the rebuilding was that of the black marble tomb of Bishop Henchman, beneath the south aisle. Another relic unearthed was a human heart 'highly spiced' in a lead cover, which was eventually reburied beneath the chancel arch. The lead coffins were removed and reinterred in the churchyard.

The parish records show that the position of the pulpit has varied over the years, conforming with prevailing doctrines. In the 18th century it was in the centre of the middle aisle, and it was a three-decker type which combined a pulpit, reader's desk and clerk's desk below. When it was moved its inlaid and carved oak panels were used to make a screen for the organist.

Until the mid–18th century church music, such as it was, was usually supplied by a wind and string band of local musicians. The introduction of organs often caused considerable ill-feeling, as chronicled by Thomas Hardy in *Under the Greenwood Tree*. In 1732 the Bishop of London gave permission for the installation of an organ at Fulham church, made by the local organ manufacturer, Benjamin Jordan. It has been rebuilt and improved a number of times since, but its original oak case has been retained, with its scroll work and cherubs and the decoration of the gold Bishop's mitre.

The church registers date from 1675 and are now kept with many others of the London area at the Greater London Record Office in Clerkenwell. A particularly interesting volume records the parish benefactors between 1622 and 1785. Faulkner apparently saw this volume in 1812, but it was then mislaid until it turned up in an office cupboard in Essex Street, Strand, in 1877. The then Vicar published a text of this volume, with notes, in 1879. (Other parish records, such as vestry minutes, poor rate assessments, and the accounts of churchwardens and overseers, are kept in the archives of Hammersmith and Fulham Libraries.)

The new church contains many of the old monuments. An elaborate memorial in the chancel records the short life of Margaret Legh, Elizabethan beauty and mother of nine children, who married at the age of sixteen and died when she was 33. Another Elizabethan lady, Katherine Hart, the eldest daughter of Sir Edward Powell who lived at Munster House, is also recorded after her death at the age of 24 in 1605. Her four children are shown with her on the memorial and the fact that one is holding a skull suggests that he predeceased her; the verse in Latin above their heads refers to 'the three cherished pledges of our chaste desire now claim the affection of their widowed sire'.

The oldest, and in many respects, the most interesting memorial is the Flemish brass, 23 inches square, now fixed to the east wall of the south aisle. Missing for many years (certainly at the time that Bowack wrote), it was discovered in 1770 by workmen digging the foundation. It depicts a head and shoulders portrait of a shrouded woman with angels on either side, above an inscription which says that she was Margaret Saunders, born in Ghent, Flanders, and who died in 1529. Dame Margaret was the wife of Gerard Hornebolt, court painter to Henry VIII, who came to England in 1528, just a year before his wife's death.

A brass to Sir William Butts, chief physician to Henry VIII, and resident of the Rectory, used to exist but there is only a stone tablet now, erected some years after his death in 1545. Numbered among his patients were Anne Boleyn, Jane Seymour, Mary Tudor and Cardinal Wolsey, and when the latter fell into disfavour Butts attempted to arrange a reconciliation with Henry VIII.

On the west wall of the Tower Chapel is a stone to the memory of Bridget Holland, wife of Henry Holland, the architect of Carlton House and the old Drury Lane Theatre; she was the daughter of the great landscape gardener Lancelot 'Capability' Brown. Not far away is a rather plain monument which Fèret nevertheless considered to be one of the finest in the church, that of Thomas Winter of Fulham House, whose claim to fame was that he had killed a tiger with his bare hands while serving as a Consul in India. He died in 1681.

All Saints churchyard miraculously maintains an air of tranquility, given the noise not a stone's throw away. Churchyards pose the dilemma – shall they be tidy or romantically decayed? So far, romance has won, but it will need to be jealously guarded if municipal tidiness is not to overcome it. Great leaning tombs and the spreading weeds and foliage may well be its undoing. At present, the churchyard is maintained by the Council's Parks Department, which is attempting to create a natural environment – a delicate operation – but with some success. An old notice in the churchyard used to say 'Do no harm, pluck no flowers, walk not on the grass, suffer no one to play...the place whereon thou standest is holy ground'. But in olden times children playing on

108. Memorial to Lady Margaret Legh in All Saints church.

the grass was the least of the problem. Pigs and other livestock could overrun the graveyard and the Court General in 1611 ordered that all inhabitants of Fulham street who 'suffered their hoggs and hoggerells to come and go into the churchyard', be fined. It was not unusual for the ground to be used to dry laundry and this formed the basis of a Vestry resolution in 1738.

The churchyard was enlarged in 1817, when eighteen old men from the workhouse were employed in laying it out, and a further addition occurred in 1843. But in March 1863 the Medical Officer of Health for Fulham, examining some well water in the immediate vicinity, found it impregnated with filtration from soil in the graveyard where interments could number nearly three hundred a year, and the graveyard was closed for new burials thenceforward.

Records of burial fees show that the charges made for use of the parish velvet pall went to the charity children. John Dwight, grandson of the potter and son of the late Vicar of Fulham, contested the heavy charges made for the interment of his daughter Millicent. He won his case, with costs, and when he died in 1745 he showed that he still bore a grudge by adding a clause to his will instructing that he should be 'decently buried upon his father's corpse, wrapped in a sheet of lead and one shilling only paid to the priest to show they impose upon the poor parishioners of Fulham.'[9] In 1783 the charge for a vault was reduced from £60 to £40. Regulations stipulated that if the cortege arrived more than ten minutes late a fine should be imposed, increasing by two shillings for every tardy ten minutes thereafter.

The early years of the 19th century were the heyday of the body-snatchers, before the 1832 Anatomy Act permitted the dissection of unclaimed pauper bodies. Fulham's quiet little graveyard was a target, along with many others, for the activities of the 'resurrection men'. Often the fear of having a corpse stolen would induce relatives to take it in turns to guard the grave at night. The last record of a snatch at Fulham was in 1828 when a corpse was removed and carried by cart to a Dr Rouse's house in Walham Green.[10]

The *Annual Register* of 1886 contained a gruesome story of a man who appears to have been buried alive in Fulham churchyard. The body of a coachman was found 'without any of the common signs of life' in a nearby stable. When the funeral was over someone insisted that during the service he had heard a rumbling and struggling from within the coffin. The earth was removed, the coffin opened, and it was found that the poor man, although now absolutely dead, had come to as his burial was taking place.

Eight Bishops lie in a plot to the east of the church, their grave generally marked by a substantial tomb and a lengthy inscription. They are in the loneliest and most atmospheric part of the churchyard. Here the tangle of growth seems inspired by the illustrious bones beneath it, so much so that the lids of some of the monuments are lifted by the greenery.

Most visitors to the churchyard are eager to see the well publicised, jokey, tombstone in memory of Isabella and Joseph Murr (Isabella, wife of a schoolmaster, died in 1802, at the age of 52). The stone has recently been restored and bears this inscription:

> Ye who possess the highest charms of life
> A tender friend – a kind indulgent wife
> Oh learn their worth. In her beneath this stone
> These pleasing attributes together shone
> Was not true happiness with them combined
> Ask the spoiled being she has left behind.
>   HE'S GONE TOO

Another interesting feature of the churchyard is an elaborate mortar excavated in Putney High Street in 1827. It is thought to have possibly been an ancient font, since it resembles one in Chester Cathedral, but this has never been authenticated.

The post of Fulham's rector was held as a sinecure. This practice (both in England and the Continent) arose when parochial endowments were vested in religious houses and prebendaries of cathedrals, which then appointed the parish priest or rector. In Fulham's case, the patronage was in the hands of the Bishop of London. It became the custom in England for the rector himself to nominate a vicar to carry out the pastoral work, while still retaining for himself a large part of the tithe revenues. A vicar was in office in Fulham by 1302 at least and it is presumed that the custom was established here by then. Often the rectors held other preferments elsewhere, and did not normally live in Fulham or play any part in its day-to-day affairs.[11]

One rector, Simon Heynes, had played a key part in the divorce of Catherine of Aragon by Henry VIII, and had also signed the decree which invalidated the king's marriage to Anne of Cleves.[12] Despite this, however, he fell foul of the Six Articles, introduced by Henry VIII in an effort to introduce uniform beliefs, and he was committed temporarily to the Fleet Prison in 1542 for lewd and seditious preaching. A successor, Thomas Darbyshire, a nephew of Bishop Bonner, also found himself in the Fleet for being pro-Catholic, and ended his days as a Catholic preacher in Lorraine.[13]

At the time of the Civil War the post of rector of Fulham was sequestered and given to the oddly named Puritan divine Adoniram Byfield,[14] who had served as a chaplain in the army of Robert, Earl of Essex, generalissimo of the Parliamentary forces. Described as a 'most zealous covenanter', he was one of two scribes appointed to compile a mode of public worship without the aid of set forms of prayer. For this he was paid four shillings a day, with the profits from the copyright. Byfield was presented with both the rectory and vicarage of Fulham by the new secular lord of the manor, Colonel Edward Harvey.

After the Civil War period and into the 18th and early 19th centuries the offices of rector and vicar of Fulham were held together, prior to the final abolition of the office of rector.

The first recorded Vicar of Fulham was named Robert; he appears in the *London and Middlesex Fines*, which note that in 1320 William de Northboro and Egidia, his wife, 'purchased certaine premises in the manor from Robert Vicar of the church of Fulham.' The vicars, just like the rectors, quite often treated their own post as a sinecure and used overworked and ill-paid curates to actually look after the parish. This allowed a priest to accept a number of vicarages. Thus, John Sudbury, who became Vicar of Fulham in 1440, held vicarages in four other parishes in Essex, plus two in London, and prebends in Holborn, Brondesbury and York, not necessarily at the same time, but most likely some of them were.[15] In contrast, Richard Stevenson, who was Vicar of Fulham at the time of the 1665 Great Plague of London, is noted in the Vestry minutes of 1667 as having performed 'assiduous work to alleviate the distress of the poor of Fulham'. His 'great pains at the time of the visitation' were rewarded with a gratuity of £5.

After the founding of the Ecclesiastical Commission in 1857 and the restructuring of the Church, sinecure appointments were abolished and vicars became full-time. One of the longest lived of Fulham vicars must have been Robert George Baker, who held the position for over 37 years until he resigned in 1871, retiring to Parsons Green, where he died seven years later in his 90th year. Baker was fascinated by the history of the parish and gave a series of lectures on its 'olden characters' as well as carrying out research into its charities and benefactors.

The church accounts were kept by a parish clerk – James Cluet, or Clewett, in 1627, is the earliest we know of. Apart from the accounts, he was responsible for washing church linen, oiling the bells and ringing them at four and eight, cleaning the church, tending the clock and keeping the register. He was paid £6 a year.

The clerk's principal officer was the beadle, an office of great antiquity, who carried out various duties such as serving writs and ensuring that no poor strangers settled in the parish (thereby becoming a charge on the poor rate); he could also act as town crier and constable. He was responsible for summoning parishioners to meetings of the Vestry and he kept order at church. For all this he was paid £4 a year and supplied with a cap, breeches and coat. John Hodnutt, a beadle who had his portrait painted in his finery in 1690, was buried in the churchyard and the parish registers recorded his interment as 'John Hudnott, gravedigger, alias 'Old Forelock', a nickname which the Vicar had crossed through.

The last Fulham beadle was Charles Griffin. He and his father before him were bakers at Walham Green from 1800 to 1850. On assuming office he discarded the usual red plush knee breeches and wore black trousers with a red cord down the seam, and a black, instead of a red, waistcoat. The coat was still a splendid affair, with dark blue cloth and heavy gold lace to which was affixed a scarlet plush cape, also decorated with two rows of gold lace. In Griffin's day the duties still involved attendance at church, but he also had care of the gas lights and 'the charge of the boys in the aisle during Divine service'. During the week he attended the vestry and other parochial meetings, even the lectures given in the schoolroom. Gradually, his duties lessened and his clothes became less distinctive.[16] When Archibald Tait, the former Bishop, returned to Fulham church as Archbishop of Canterbury, he noted in his diary 'Very few faces in the church which I recollect – Griffin the Beadle, despoiled by modern parochial economy of his splendid garments'.[17] The post died, with Griffin, in 1884.

NOTES ON SOURCES

1   Feret, Vol I, pp201, 202.
2   Miss A.H. Bracken, *A Guide to Fulham Parish Church*, (1936, rev. Dennis Haselgrove 1973), p3.
3   John Strype, *Life of Aylmer* (1701), p97.
4   Feret, Vol I, p159.
5   Miscellaneous Book Vol 498, pp8–10, Public Record Office; Feret, Vol I, pp176–183.
6   The Will of Dr Thomas Edwardes, 9 January 1619, codicil 13 January 1619.
7   Feret, Vol I, p174.
8   Bracken, p8.
9   The Will of John Dwight, 3 October 1745.
10 Feret, Vol I, pp280–283.
11 *Ibid.*, Vol II, pp8–25.
12 *Ibid.*, Vol II, p13.
13 *Ibid.*, Vol II, p15.
14 *Ibid.*, Vol II, p18.
15 *Ibid.*, Vol II, p27.
16 *Ibid.*, Vol II, pp1–4.
17 Davidson and Benham, *Life of Archbishop Tait* (1891), Vol II, p524.

CHAPTER THIRTEEN

Centuries of Change

In 1634 the number of rated households in Fulham was 121, most of them near the parish church.[1] Ninety years later, in 1724, there were 445 dwellings, representing a population of 2225 people, a figure which was to increase fivefold over the next century. By 1851, over eleven thousand people lived in Fulham village, Walham Green, North End and Fulham Fields, mostly work-men and labourers, only a quarter of whom had been born in the district.[2]

The increase in population, as elsewhere in London, exacerbated the problem of sewage disposal. Fulham's first Medical Officer of Health, F.J. Burge, was faced with the troubles caused by a profusion of open ditches, filthy sewers and cess pits. Over thirty years Fulham's sewage system was improved and connected to the main London system, designed by the great Victorian engineer, Joseph Bazalgette.

Fulham may still have been rural in 1851, but conditions were far from idyllic. Large numbers of Irish labourers worked in the 'noted land of cabbages' at Fulham Fields, maintaining large families on poor wages; their living condi-tions were pitiful and the infant mortality rate was high. Apart from the building trades, where work was beginning to expand, there was also employ-ment in the new gas works, where foul fumes made life unpleasant and unhealthy, and in the breweries, foundries and small workshops.

The Poor Law Amendment Act 1834 established the Guardians of the Poor, who took over the duties once performed by parishes and vestries in caring for the poor.'Outdoor' relief (that given to people in their own homes) was substituted by workhouses. Whole families were housed and fed in institutions where those who could work were employed in menial and dreary tasks. For economy 'Unions' of parishes built large workhouses. Fulham, Hammersmith, Kensington, Chelsea and Paddington were grouped together for this purpose, but this policy was rarely a success and many unions broke up. Chelsea, Paddington and Kensington all went their own way and Fulham and Hammersmith were left to plan their own building in Fulham Palace Road, later to become Fulham Infirmary, on the site of the present Charing Cross Hospital.

Many inner suburbs, such as Fulham, resembled a large building site in the 19th century, as new estates were built. Photographs of some areas of Fulham in the 1870s portray the drab ugliness of the buildings, and a prolifera-tion of hoardings and billboards. Most things would have been painted brown or black to hide, as much as possible, the coating of grime coming from the chimneys of houses and factories.

The problems of Fulham, familiar in other suburbs, of uncontrolled de-velopment, smoke and fume emissions, overcrowding, poor sewage systems and inadequate clean water supplies, were partly the result of poor London government. While other large cities were able to govern themselves London, outside the City, was fragmented into tiny units, a situation that the City, jealous of the appointment of an all-London authority which would rival it, encouraged. However, the Metropolitan Management Act of 1855 set up 38 local authorities in London, combining old parishes into larger areas, with a Metropolitan Board of Works, whose function initially was to sort out the sewage system of the metropolis, but whose duties later transformed the

The GRANVILLE

Walham Green.

Manager   -   Mr. R. W. Duce.

MONDAY, APRIL 29th, 1912,

and Twice Nightly during the week at 6.20 & 9.10.

IN AID OF THE

"TITANIC" SUFFERERS

SPECIAL MATINEE on THURSDAY, MAY 2, the proceeds of which will be forwarded to the Lord Mayor's Fund.   Doors Open 2 p.m., commence 2.30.   POPULAR PRICES, 1s. to 3d.

G. H. ELLIOTT

The Original Chocolate Coloured Coon.

VIOLET STOCKELLE.   LARRY LEWIS.

THE O'HANLON TRIO.

SIG. & MDME. BORELLI.   JOHNNY DWYER.

LILLIE LASSAH.

CINEMATOGRAPH, Showing New Pictures.

VICTORIA CAMPBELL, Scottish Nightingale.

WALTER ELLIS and his London Company will present THE

'SLEEPWALKER'

Friday, May 10th, Mr. Bob Duce's Third Grand Complimentary Benefit. On this occasion One Performance only. Grand Star Programme. See Special Bills. Book your seats at once.

109. Advertisement for fund raising evenings at the Granville Theatre in aid of those affected by the Titanic disaster. From the Fulham Chronicle, 26 April, 1912.

capital and led eventually to the creation of the London County Council. In this rearrangement Fulham and Hammersmith were grouped together, with offices in Hammersmith. (History was to repeat itself in 1965 when these very boroughs were grouped together in the enlarged London area and the London Borough of Hammersmith and Fulham was created.)

Parliamentary reform followed. Fulham, previously grouped with Hammersmith, Kensington and Chelsea, to return two members to Parliament, was made a separate constituency and in 1885 returned its own member, the Conservative William H. Fisher.

After Fulham had sought, by virtue of its greater population, increased representation on the District Board of Hammersmith and Fulham, the Board was abolished and the two vestries resumed responsibility for their respective areas in 1886. At this time local authorities were encouraged and empowered to take on more responsibilities in the fields of social welfare, improvements in roads and street lighting, and the provision of public baths, laundries and libraries. The new Fulham Vestry inherited the Board's refuse carts and horses, but land by the riverside on which rubbish could be dumped while awaiting transportation by barge, was becoming increasingly scarce. It was to be another 15 years before a Destruction Station, which burnt the refuse, was opened at Townmead Road.

The Vestry still had no proper meeting place and convened in school rooms and church halls until the building of the Town Hall in 1890. It had to deal with the problems caused by the hard winters of 1886 and 1887, which brought great unemployment. Builders, market gardeners and others whose business was in the open air, were laid off. There was no dole and long queues would form outside the vestry offices in Walham Green, hoping for casual work sweeping snow. It was not until 1902 that local authorities were required to set up Labour Exchanges.

Those drab days for the poor, at the end of that century and in the early years of the Edwardian age, were only occasionally relieved by the brief pleasures of celebration of national events, such as the Diamond Jubilee of the Queen's coronation in 1897, when thousands of Fulham children converged on the garden of Beaufort House for what was commonly known as a 'bunfight', organised by the Vestry; later they departed with enamel Jubilee mugs and bags containing half a pound of seed or sultana cake. The *Fulham Chronicle* reported that although everyone had had a good time, the event ended in a typically English downpour of rain.[5] At the coronation of Edward VII in 1902, a dinner 'for the poor' was provided in Bishops Park. About 13,000 people attended, although this was far less than half of the estimated 34,000 residents living in poverty. The church bells rang and the dinner was attended by the Prince and Princess of Wales (the future George V and Queen Mary). The feast included 10,000 pounds of beef, 15,000 pounds of plum pudding, 1,000 bottles of Yorkshire Relish, 10,000 loaves of bread, 15 barrels of beer and 2,000 bottles of lager, with a special Temperance Table set up so that the teetotallers should not be upset by the smell of the beer.[6]

National party labels had not yet invaded local government. The candidates in Fulham were either Progressives or Moderates, the former 'neither Conservative, Liberal or Socialist', the latter nearer to the Conservatives. The first election resulted in a narrow majority for the Progressives, who lived up to their name with a pioneer venture in municipal enterprise, the opening of the Fulham Electric Lighting and Dust Destruction Station at Townmead Road, although this scheme had actually been originated by a resolution, four years earlier, of the old vestry. The power station was ingeniously fed, not only by coal, but by refuse. This enterprise remained in the hands of the local authority until nationalisation.

In the sweeping national Liberal victory of the 1906 General Election, the

Welsh draper, Timothy Davies, now well established at Walham Green, entered politics as a supporter of Lloyd George. His election as MP for Fulham,
with promises of widespread social reforms, must have caused rejoicing in the
nearby 'Avenues', Rock, Walham, Grove and Lodge, regarded as being among
the worst slums in the neighbourhood. The Medical Officer of Health considered that drink was one of the main causes of squalor in these run-down,
seedy, multi-occupied houses, and certainly many of their occupants worked
in the nearby Swan Brewery (Stansfield's), where payment in kind with cheap
beer did not encourage sobriety.

*110. The Diamond Jubilee celebrations
of the West London Band of Hope
Union, at Fulham Town Hall in 1936.*

   Social reforms did not please everyone and the introduction of national
insurance against sickness and unemployment was described in a report by
Fulham's Guardians of the Poor as 'a serious danger to the whole community'
which they feared 'would now become experts in malingering'.[7]

   Timothy Davies was ousted in 1910 by his old opponent, the Conservative, William Fisher. At this time the cost of living was rising, there were rail
and dock strikes, and in 1912 the miners joined the protest. The Coronation in
1910 provided a brief distraction, especially for the children. In London, they
were treated to a special King's Fete at the Crystal Palace; 3,400 went from
Fulham. Those unlucky in the ballot for invitations were placated by a party at
Fulham Palace. Joy's, the Dawes Road baker, made 14,300 cakes for free
distribution.[8]

   The Education Act of 1870 established the London School Board and the
great age of school building began. For the purposes of education Fulham was
united with Chelsea and the first Board schools, albeit in temporary accom-

111. North End Road School in 1911.

modation, were opened in Harwood Road and William (now Earsby) Street in the south and north. Between 1880 and 1890 ten more were built in Fulham, the first being in Star Lane (Greyhound Road), now sold to become a private Law College.

The population grew to over 137,000 by 1901 and this encouraged a new spate of school building. In 1902 the London County Council took over education and at the same time Secondary Schools were established to provide free places for the more promising elementary school children from the age of fourteen.

It was a practical age in which schooling was generally regarded as no more than a grounding for wage earning at the earliest possible moment. The study of school log books reveals unexpected refinements, however. At Ackmar Road, the dedication of two teacher sisters, 'the Miss Moores', is still remembered by some of their surviving (very elderly) pupils, who recall a practice flat for the teaching of domestic science, drill and skipping, and magic lantern shows. At Peterborough School there was a special section for invalid children in the care of a trained nurse, and the syllabus included not only football and swimming, but tennis and a violin band. Nature notes recorded that a nightingale had been heard singing in South Park.

Highlights of the school year were Empire Day, with its patriotic songs and parades (most schools began the day saluting the Union Jack), and the crowning of the May Queen: 'the most wonderful day of my life', wrote a little girl after her turn had come.[9]

112. Sherbrook Road Higher Grade Girls' School, c1902–5.

113. Star Road School in 1910.

114. A piano shop, Hanes & Co., 578 Fulham Road, c1902–11.

Central schools were an innovation in state education, in the 1920s, to provide commercial or trade education for bright pupils who showed interest in academic subjects or, more likely, whose parents wanted them to become wage earners at an earlier age than they would have done had they been at a secondary school. Sadly, many of the older boys who attended Fulham's schools in 1911, would not live to be employed in the 1920s. The Great War came.

NOTES ON SOURCES

1   Feret, Vol I, pp28–29.
2   Hasker, p89.
3   Feret, Vol I, pp14–15; Vol III, p321.
4   Hasker, pp97–98.
5   *Fulham Chronicle* Centenary Supplement, April 1988, pB.
6   *Fulham as it Was* (Hendon Publishing Co 1983), p64.
7   Hasker, p155.
8   *Ibid.*, p154.
9   *Peterborough School Magazine* 1908 (Fulham Central Library).

CHAPTER FOURTEEN
Getting from Here to There

In medieval times the lord of the manor was responsible for the upkeep of roads and from time to time was allowed to levy tolls of 'pavage' for their repair. Larger property owners were required by statute to supply labour, transport and materials for the work involved. A Surveyor of the Highways was chosen from among the tenants each year to supervise the work and to inspect the roads. No wonder that the mid–17th century roads were in an appalling condition. The government's solution was the encouragement of turnpike trusts, private bodies which maintained main roads and were allowed to charge a toll to users. One of the first such trusts to operate in Fulham controlled the road from Knightsbridge to Fulham Ferry. Tolls varied from sixpence for a coach drawn by six horses, to fivepence for a score of calves, sheep or lambs; the royal carriages and their Horse Guards were exempt.

Toll gates or bars existed between Chaldon House and Fulham Charity Schools in Fulham High Street on the present approach to Putney Bridge, at the entrance to Fulham Park by Elysium Row (in New King's Road), and opposite the Swan at Walham Green. Others were at the northern end of Burlington Road, at Percy Cross (in Fulham Road near Parsons Green), opposite Munster House (Fulham Road-Munster Road junction), opposite Sussex House in Fulham Palace Road, and opposite the Bell and Anchor in Hammersmith Road.[1]

Generally, toll roads were unpopular. The trusts, it was said, erected too many toll bars, and the roads were still described as 'impassable, never watered or washed, lighted or paved.' With few exceptions the tollgate system was abolished in 1865.

Fulham escaped much railway development. Its geographical situation within a loop of the Thames kept it outside the main routes to central London and the consequent disruption of 'cut and cover' railway building, the tracks being mainly above ground or on viaducts. (It is interesting that even in modern times London Transport trains only cross the Thames in west London at Putney and Kew, thus leaving places such as Barnes outside the tube system.)

In April 1869 the Metropolitan District Railway extended its line from Gloucester Road to West Brompton and this was further lengthened in 1880 to Putney Bridge via Walham Green and Parsons Green. And in 1869 also, a link to Kensington (Addison Road) was opened, with West Kensington (North End) reached in 1874.

The Great Northern and Piccadilly and Brompton line was extended to Hammersmith in 1905 and Barons Court Station opened the same year.[2] The trains were unlike the silver 'cigar tubes' of today, being partially open, with chain link gates to admit passengers, operated by the guards.

Fulham may have been rather badly served by railways but it made up for it with buses for, with its neighbour Hammersmith, it provided offices for dozens of small bus companies and stables for the hundreds of horses. The French-owned London General Omnibus Company, in its attempt to unify and monopolise, bought many small companies and routes, which included that from Putney to London Bridge via Fulham. The rival London District Omnibus Company flew Union Jacks on its vehicles to emphasise its English

115. *A horse bus shown between the Arab Boy and Putney Bridge station. View from Putney Bridge.*

116. *A lorrybus in service on the No. 11 route in 1919.*

117. *Construction of West Brompton Metropolitan District Railway station in 1867.*

118. *West Brompton Station.*

119. Last Train from Walham Green Station – a satirical postcard of c1908.

120. A Vanguard motor bus of the London Motor Omnibus Company, c1906.

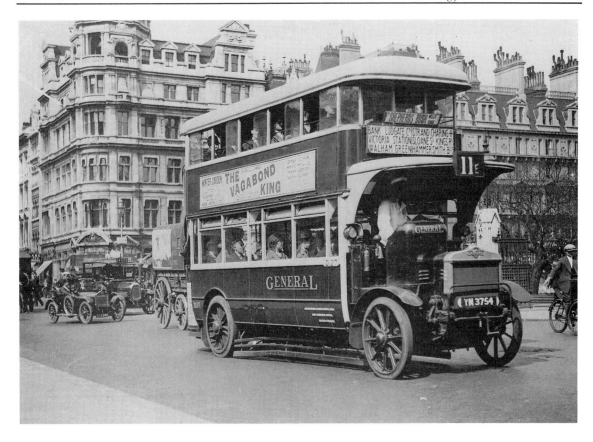

121. General bus of 1926.

origins. Its buses were equipped with 'garden seats' facing forwards, as opposed to the knife board design where passengers sat back-to-back on the top deck. The journey, from Putney to London Bridge, a distance of 7½ miles, took eighty minutes; the buses ran every fifteen minutes and the fare was sixpence.[3]

Buses were distinguished by their colours rather than by route numbers – white from Liverpool Street to Fulham, red to Hammersmith, and so on. Tickets were not issued until 1891 and then there was a strike of bus conductors who demanded higher wages if they were to be deprived of the perks which the non-ticket system allowed.

It was decided that the narrow streets of Fulham were unsuitable for tramways. Only one route operated in the area, along the Fulham Palace Road, and this was replaced by a trolley bus route in the 1930s, itself withdrawn in 1962.

Farm Lane in particular was a popular area for bus company depots. The London General had stables in Bramber, Estcourt, Greyhound, Hurlingham and Normand Roads. The London Car Company occupied two sites in Star Road, one of which, now used for sheltered housing, was later taken over by the London Co-operative Society as a warehouse. Smaller companies had catchier names, such as the Red Rover based at Parsons Green, the Omega from Farm Lane, the Celtic, the Universal, the Eagle, the Chariot and 'Our Bus'.

The increased use of roads caused many problems for the Vestry. Roads might be cobbled and noisy whereas it was much preferred to have them made of wood blocks soaked in creosote, because they were quieter. (In 1890 residents of Farm Lane petitioned for their street to be wood paved owing to the noise of the horses using the stables there.)

As the small bus garages closed, taxis moved into the Farm Lane area: Fulham's side streets still have more than the average number of repair garages. The horse, of course, had gone with the exception of those pulling coal carts and milk floats, or those owned by rag and bone dealers; these survived until the years immediately following the last war. I do not know now of a stable in Fulham. In 1914 hundreds of the patient beasts that pulled the buses were sent out to Flanders, and in the early days of September 1939, West Kensington residents recall seeing a cavalcade of dray horses moving in the blackout with a few, flickering torchlights: presumably they had been found some military task even in those more mechanised times.

NOTES ON SOURCES

1 Feret, Vol I, p39.
2 *How we used to Travel* (Fulham and Hammersmith Libraries 1979), p16.
3 *Ibid.*, p5.
4 *Ibid.*, p6 .

CHAPTER FIFTEEN
Wars, Peace and Politics

A 91-year-old Fulham woman recalls the summer day of 4 August 1914, when she was enjoying an open-air band concert at the Earl's Court Exhibition by a German orchestra. Abruptly the music stopped and the bandmaster announced: 'Ladies and Gentlemen, War has been declared.' The musicians silently filed off the bandstand.

German bands and bakeries were popular features of London life in the first decade of this century – the former would not be heard again for many years and the latter suffered frequent humiliation and persecution, specially when wartime events, such as the sinking of the *Lusitania* in May 1915, aroused particular resentment. On that occasion, angry crowds stoned the bakers' windows, although one of them, in Filmer Road, managed to placate the mob with free bread and cakes.[1]

Within days of the declaration of war the local territorial regiments were in evidence. Recruits soon outnumbered supplies of uniforms and many of the new soldiers were issued instead with navy-blue uniforms provided by the Salvation Army. Recruiting offices were opened at Fulham Town Hall and the secondary school at Fulham Cross. Lord Kitchener's pointing finger encouraged many men, not all motivated by patriotism, but also by unemployment. Even local horses from the bus stables and coal yards were shipped to haul wagons in Flanders.

The Bishop of London of the time, Arthur Winnington Ingram, was an enthusiastic patriot and voluntary recruiting officer, even crossing the Archbishop of Canterbury in advocating that priests should forsake their parishes and enlist for active service.[2] He was also Honorary Chaplain of the Rifle Brigade and visited it in France, where he took services under fire and celebrated Holy Communion in dug-outs.[3]

The Prince of Wales launched a National Relief Fund to help wives and mothers left behind virtually penniless, and it was a common sight to see children waiting at the gates of Hurlingham and Bishops Park, where their fathers were camped, to collect from them their share of the 'King's shilling'.

Patriotic recruitment did not go unopposed. The passing of the National Registration Act 1915, which obliged every man to submit his name, address, age and ability to do war work, provoked a meeting of conscientious objectors at Dawes Road.[4] Patriotism did wear thinner, however, everywhere, and after the lack of success of another recruiting campaign, conscription was introduced for men aged between 18 and 40.

The first air-raids on London were in 1915. Precautions took the form of police and boy scouts touring the streets bearing sandwich-board placards saying 'Take Cover' and blowing whistles. Similar boards declared 'All Clear'. There were black-out regulations, although nowhere near as stringent as in the 2nd World War. Householders had to dim their lights, and stallholders in the market used oil lights or candles instead of the flaring naphtha lamps.[5]

Princess Louise attended a 'Hints for Housewives' meeting in Fulham at which it was suggested that the rich should eat more expensive food to leave more bread for the poor! Although the Public Meals Order restricted the portions of meat to be served in restaurants to two and a half ounces, and 'treating' in pubs was forbidden, food remained officially unrationed until the

122. Nos. 555–561 Fulham Road, c1916–18. The Army Recruiting Office is on the left.

last months of the war. However, some local authorities drew up their own rules: the Hammersmith Food Committee prepared a scheme to ration various commodities and butchers were instructed not to sell more than 5lbs of meat to any one household.[6] Ugly scenes occurred in North End Road towards the end of the war when shoppers clashed with traders, and mounted police were enlisted to control long queues. The Bishop of London was persuaded to allow allotments on the grounds of the Palace.[7] At the end of the war, when these were due to be relinquished, he told the gardeners that they could stay on, but he would have to raise the rent – from ten shillings to a pound a year. They greeted the news with a cheer and the Bishop liked to tell how he was the only landlord who could double rents and *still* be told he was a jolly good fellow! These allotments are still used by a new generation of gardeners.

The *Fulham Chronicle* of the time records the dreadful lists of local casualties at the battles of the Somme, Ypres and Passchendale.[8] Fulham Infirmary, transformed into a military hospital, cared for many of the wounded, and photographs show large, formal groups of patients wearing the official bright blue 'wounded' suits and red ties, with their nurses looking more like nuns in their flowing white head dresses.

What with the food shortages and the slaughter, the tide of enthusiasm for the war turned and public patience reached breaking point. In August 1918 bus and train workers and the police went on strike, and a Spanish influenza epidemic added to the depression. The Armistice, signed on 11 November 1918, came none too soon.

Fulham's Conservative Member of Parliament, William Fisher, retained his seat until 1918, when he was appointed President of the Local Government Board set up to administer the recent Electoral Reform Act in preparation for the first post-war General Election in December. Under this new Act, which reorganised constituency boundaries and enfranchised women over thirty who were householders or married to one, Fulham was divided into two seats – East and West. Fisher, in fact, lost his seat at the election, accused (unjustly according to *The Times*) of failing to have the new electoral registers ready in time. This was an undignified end to a career and he died two years later, by then ennobled as Baron Downham.

123. Fulham Military Hospital, c1915. The men are wearing hospital 'blues'.

His place in local politics was taken by a former Mayor, Henry Norris, builder and estate agent who, with his partner, had been responsible for much of the development of the farmlands at Crabtree. Mayor from 1909, he was knighted in 1917 and stood for the new seat of Fulham East, becoming an MP in the new Coalition under the continuing premiership of Lloyd George; he was cast aside by his party in 1922 in favour of Colonel Kenyon Vaughan Morgan. Fulham West was represented by another Conservative, Sir Cyril Cobb, commemorated now in Cobb's Hall in Fulham Palace Road, who, except for a brief period, held the seat until his death in 1938.

In the 1919 local elections the Labour Party won twice as many seats as the Municipal Reform Party (a name for various Conservatives) – in London generally Labour took control of 16 of the 28 boroughs. In Fulham the new Council, which included women for the first time, dispensed with outmoded procedures, ceremonial robes and much protocol. It proposed, to the dismay of many, the purchase of the Hurlingham Club grounds on which to build housing. The Ministry of Health blocked the plan by refusing powers of compulsory purchase.[9]

Some problems did not go away once the war had finished. Slums were prevalent and good housing at low rents was scarce in Fulham. Then again, as elsewhere, unemployment was growing at an alarming rate. Only two months after a memorial to the 1100 Fulham men who had died in the war was unveiled, an angry mob of unemployed ex-servicemen stormed a public meeting at the Town Hall. It was led, according to the *Fulham Chronicle*, by a Communist anarchist called Hanson, protesting against the post-war lack of homes and jobs.[10] In July 1924, when the Council issued closing orders on four old and unsafe cottages in Vanston Place at Fulham Broadway, the occupants refused to move and their belongings were carried out to the street by bailiffs. No alternative accommodation was offered the residents and an impromptu open-air meeting nearby demanded housing for the families involved, which numbered forty people. A march to the the Town Hall procured accommodation for the homeless in the Town Hall itself, but the demonstration was not appeased and mounted police were called to disperse it.[11]

A report issued by the social centre in Lillie Road, Bishop Creighton House, soon after the General Strike of 1926, stated that very few of Fulham's houses were in single family occupation. Many houses shared cooking facilities on the landings, and an outside lavatory; most had no bath. The Bishop of London was instrumental in founding the Fulham Housing Association in 1927 and the Fulham Housing Improvement Society, the latter of which bought houses, improved them and then let them to local families. It also built flats at Parsons Green Lane (Rosamonds) and Clancarty Road (Brightwells).[12] The borough council bought the old Swan Brewery site in Fulham Road in 1929 for local authority housing (Fulham Court). The Bishop also added his name to a Labour Party manifesto in 1928 which stated that there were houses in Fulham where 'water streams down the walls, floors are so rotten that the furniture legs fall through...' Between the wars over 23,000 people left Fulham to seek housing elsewhere.

Still unemployment persisted as a local issue. A Council meeting was interrupted in 1931 by the Unemployed Workers Movement and two months later the *Fulham Chronicle* reported 'exciting struggles' in which police and citizens were injured near Walham Green Employment Exchange, after the protesters had ignored a ban on demonstrations near employment exchanges. Meanwhile, the new National Government had introduced even more austere measures, including the Means Test for assistance.[13] Late in 1931 the Conservatives regained the country and Fulham Council. But it was a volatile political time. In August 1932, at a by-election in Fulham, the Labour candidate, John Wilmot, campaigning on a Peace ticket, overturned the Conservative majority of 15,000 and replaced it with one of 5,000 for himself. His triumph was proclaimed as a 'victory for peace, disarmament and no food taxes'. But the pacifist vote was probably as much due to a popular feeling that public funds should be devoted to housing rather than to guns in those difficult days between the wars, than to anything else. Some people have said that this by-election delayed re-armament for three years, and if this is so, Fulham has much to answer for. This theory was denied by the late (Lord) Michael Stewart MP, who, in his biography, declared that 'governments are not so easily swayed on major issues.'

The Labour swing continued in the 1934 LCC elections – all four Fulham seats were won by them and in the same year the Party won Fulham Council as well. Members of that radical council included the first woman mayor for Fulham, Alice Gilliatt, and Professor Harold Laski of the London School of Economics, who lived in Addison Bridge Place. From this era date council flats named after Keir Hardie, Robert Owen, Mary McArthur, William Morris and Holman Hunt.

The mood of militant pacifism evaporated. John Wilmot lost his seat in

124. (Opposite, top) The back view of Chelmsford Street, c1931.

125. (Opposite, bottom) Rock Avenue, c1931.

126. Hockfield Place, 1931.

127. Nos. 555–563 Fulham Road, with the Town Hall on the far left.

1935 and the Labour council co-operated in measures to counter air-bombardment. Fear and anticipation of a new war overshadowed such royal events as the Jubilee of George V and the coronation of George VI and their consequent local celebrations. In 1938 the disused Maternity Hospital in Fulham Road was taken over for an ARP centre and depots were selected for the storage of gas masks; Anderson shelters in their thousands were delivered to householders; air raid posts were established at Parsons Green and on Eel Brook Common where, in May 1939, a mock emergency was staged to train the ARP members. The countdown to war had begun, oddly enough at a time when West Fulham had, to much surprise, elected a new pacifist MP, Dr Edith Summerskill, whose name was to be very well known after the war.

A thousand houses and flats in Fulham were destroyed in the bombing which ensued and another 30,000 damaged.[15]

The first bomb to fall on Fulham was at 3am on 9 September, 1940 at 132 St Dunstan's Road, followed very shortly by a direct hit on Fulham Hospital. Half an hour later the turbine house of Fulham Power Station was hit, where there were casualties. That first night ten ARP rescue workers died when a delayed action bomb exploded as they were trying to rescue families at the junction of Munster and St Dionis Roads. On 13 September a bomb struck a large air raid shelter in Bucklers Alley, (now the site of the Brunswick Boys' Club), killing 38 people and injuring many more. That weekend, after an enemy bomber had

SPEND WITH
OTHERS —
THAT OTHERS
MAY SPEND
WITH YOU

HALF the Unemployment
in FULHAM is in the
Building Trade......why not
put in hand your domes-
tic or business renovations
immediately?

THE FULHAM
UNEMPLOYMENT
SCHEME
(WORK AND WELFARE)

128. A leaflet re help for the unemployed.

been shot down, the body of its pilot was found in Munster Road. In his pocket was an aerial photograph of Fulham Gas Works, with a list of local key targets.[16] In September, also, the corner of Kensington Hall Gardens and North End Road was hit.

Particular targets included the area of Olympia, where the marshalling yards were, and the riverside of gasworks and power station. Two gas workers were awarded George Medals and three others the BEM for their courage in shutting off valves at the gasworks during an air raid; a bomb intended for the works hit a shelter at William Parnell House, killing four people. Few people now are aware that the colliers owned by the Electricity Department of the Borough of Fulham played a vital part in keeping the 'home fires burning', together with the ships of the various gas companies, including the Gas Light & Coke Company based also at Fulham: there was no other way than water transport to bring in the huge tonnage of coal needed for power supplies.[17] On the night of 25–26 September, 52 high explosive bombs fell on Fulham. The West Kensington area suffered particularly that night. A parachute mine in October 1940 destroyed a huge area in the vicinity of Lillie Road and Mulgrave Road. In November 1943 a bomb fell on a crowded dance hall in Putney High Street, killing over a hundred people, many of whom, mostly young women, came from Fulham. On 20 February 1944, Fulham was battered once again by a severe air raid which caused a large fire at the Queen's Club. Once again Barons Court and West Kensington suffered badly. Riverside areas from Hammersmith to Townmead were hit on 23 February, when heavy bombs struck Skelwith Road and Chancellors Road. A container of incendiaries landed on a

129. The Home Guard, No. 12 Platoon C Company of the Fulham Battalion, in Dec 1940. It was formed from the staff of the Drayton Paper Works, formerly in Sulivan Road.

shelter in Rosaville Road, killing five people. Fifty-five people died in Fulham that night.

The first flying bomb to hit Fulham was on 18 June, 1944, when Lintaine Grove – a street just to the south of old St Katharine's Convent, was badly damaged. That same day St Mary's Church, Hammersmith Road was destroyed. The last bomb to fall in Fulham was a V1 rocket, which struck Beaumont Crescent just before midnight on 2 August, 1944. Seven people were killed and nearly thirty were seriously injured.

Some five hundred Fulham civilians were killed in the bombing. At least ninety were never identified and were buried in a common grave at the cemetery in Sheen where a Garden of Remembrance was dedicated in October 1949.

Politically, after the war, Fulham remained to the left. Captain Michael Stewart joined Edith Summerskill as a Fulham MP and held his seat until he went to the Lords in 1979. The new Council built housing with much energy. A very large estate was built off Lillie Road, each block named after Labour Party personalities; an old dream was realised eventually when one of the polo grounds at Hurlingham was purchased and on its site Sulivan Court built. The LCC bought some of the rest of the grounds and laid out a park.

Another pre-war dream had come true in 1942 with the completion of the bridge which carried the Cromwell Road across the railway. Later, it was to continue, along Talgarth Road (the north side of which was demolished) and Colet Gardens, to the new Hammersmith Flyover. In the sixties a further move to build an overpass at North End Road came to naught.

Local politics and much else changed in 1965 when London's boroughs were reorganised. The old villages of Fulham and Hammersmith were reunited, at first with just the name Hammersmith but later with Fulham added – a sop to civic pride, which resented the upstart Hammersmith appearing to swallow the old parent village. In recent years Fulham has achieved some political importance as a 'marginal' Parliamentary seat, such as in 1986, when a by-election followed the death of its Conservative MP. The national media turned fully upon the result – a short-lived Labour victory as the seat swung back to the Tories in the General Election the following year. More importantly, the nature of Fulham's population has altered. As people found Chelsea too expensive so they have bought into Fulham; the trend throughout central London, of renovating and reselling for largish sums what were previously thought to be modest properties, has swept through Fulham too. Conservation Areas are now commonplace and Fulham's older and more desirable buildings are now the concern of the newly-formed Historic Building-ings Group, which hopes to co-operate with the local authority in compiling a survey of significant buildings in the borough. Landscape gardening, tree planting and general conservation are also supervised by the Hammersmith and Fulham Amenity Trust.

This care and conservation comes none too soon, for it is very easy for perfectly decent buildings to be spoilt by development, neglect or addition. For example, the mansion flats of Queen's Club Gardens, designed by Henry Gibbs, were rescued from decay caused by leaking roofs and dry rot, by a £2½million grant.

Despite 'gentrification' the most striking change in the character of Fulham since the end of the war must be the influx of immigrants, not only from the Third World but from Europe. The Polish community had already established a settlement in the West Kensington area early in the war, which has survived into the third and fourth generation, but local authority officials of even fifty years ago would have been astonished to learn that public information would need to be produced in at least ten different languages including Urdu, Cantonese and Bengali. Fulham's Carnival, a post-war institution, is nevertheless still a very 'village' affair, even if the sound of steel bands and music from other lands booms out over Fulham's small parks, the newest of which has actually been named for the West Indian political activist, Marcus Garvey.

Difficult though it can be, adaptation to ethnic change comes second to the current pressing problems of traffic congestion and transport. With so many major routes crossing it the borough has one of the worst road situations in London. It is feared this will now be aggravated by the Channel Tunnel, which temporarily prompted serious consideration of the West London Environmental Route (WEIR) along the border with Kensington and Chelsea.

Concern for the future can have a unifying effect which cuts across the barriers of race, class and politics. Whether this will prove the saviour of Fulham, only time will tell.

NOTES ON SOURCES

1   *Fulham Chronicle* Centenary Supplement, April 1988, pD.
2   Hasker, p159.
3   S.C. Carpenter, *Winnington Ingram: a biography* (1949), pp283–291.
4   Hasker, p162.
5   *Ibid.*, p159.
6   Barbara Denny, *Kensington News* Centenary Supplement, 1969, p31.
7   Hasker, pp165, 167.
8   *Fulham Chronicle* files 1914–1918.
9   Hasker, p171.
10 *Fulham Chronicle* Centenary Supplement, April 1988, pE.
11 *Ibid.*
12 Hasker, pp178–179.
13 *Fulham Chronicle* Centenary Supplement, April 1988, pF.
14 Hasker, pp196, 198.
15 A record of specific wartime incidents can be found in Hasker's *Fulham in the Second World War* (Fulham and Hammersmith Historical Society, 1984).
16 *Co-Partners' Magazine,* published by the Gas Light & Coke Company, Oct 1945.
17 C.M. Bates, *The Thames on Fire* (1985), pp130–134. Other details taken from personal diaries of the author. Detailed accounts of political and social change in the years between the two World Wars are included in Leslie Hasker's *The Place which is called Fulanham* (Fulham and Hmamersmith Historical Society 1981).

POSTSCRIPT

Fèret – Fulham's Historian

No history of Fulham should be without tribute to Charles James Fèret, whose research into the area's past has been the basis for every student since. But his very thoroughness has denied him the popular acclaim he deserves. Modern readers are not given to wading through volumes of detail, even though Fèret had considerably reduced the assembly of facts to cram into his *Fulham Old and New*, published in 1900.

Born in Goswell Street, Clerkenwell, on 19 December 1854, the son of a haberdasher, this studious man with a frail demeanour stemming from a nervous rather than a physical cause, was already a serious enough researcher at the age of twenty-one to obtain a British Museum Library ticket, just after he had been appointed second clerk in the India Office. When he was 26 he became a Fellow of the Royal Geographical Society, the same year, 1880, that his mother moved their home from West Cromwell Road, Earl's Court, to one of Gibbs and Flews' new houses, no. 49, Edith Road, West Kensington, a house bombed during the last war and now replaced by flats.

Although still employed by the India Office, Charles Fèret took up a part-time job as editor of a new local newspaper, the *Fulham Chronicle*. The main object of the paper was said to be the interests of local ratepayers, but Fèret contributed a column of local history under the pseudonym of 'Our Local Antiquary'. The first issue of this appeared in April 1888, but that was still a decade or so away from the completion of his mammoth history of Fulham.

'I am going to chat about the history of our parish, its old residents and old houses and recall a few of the curious anecdotes touching Fulham in the past,' he told *Chronicle* readers. This modest intention was far removed from the research he undertook for his *Fulham Old and New*. He wrote afterwards of his 'arduous labours necessary to secure absolute correctness. Like Boswell, I have sometimes been obliged to run half over London in order to fix a date correctly.' His researches involved the inspection of the church registers from 1675, the accounts of the churchwardens and the Overseers of the Poor from 1625, the whole of the court rolls of the manor of Fulham from 1392 (a task which took him 18 months), and searches at the Probate Registry for Wills. He was also to be found at the Public Record Office, the Bodleian Library and the British Museum, and he also researched deeds, documents and diaries in private hands.

Fèret made his intention to write his history known in the *Chronicle* early on in the paper's life. He worked in long hand, making many alterations and amendments, and the final manuscript totalled no less than 27 volumes, which, even allowing for the smaller amount of space taken up by typesetting, shows just how much further editing was done before publication. Although he received encouragement from most people his project was by no means entirely welcomed. Bishop John Jackson, for example, was very difficult about photographing Fulham Palace, although his successor, Mandell Creighton, made up for this.

Fèret's book was published by the Leadenhall Press, a firm renowned for such productions. *Fulham Old and New* consisted of three volumes, about the size of modern telephone directories, with a total of nearly 1,000 pages. They were illustrated with prints and contemporary photographs (he used three local photographers for his work), some sketch plans, a few family trees, and three maps. The work was dedicated to Bishop Creighton and published by subscription, a popular method at the time, which ensured a certain guaranteed sale. The subscribers included many notable residents, businesses and institutions such as the Burne-Jones family, Miss Charlotte Sulivan, John Barker's of Kensington and William Whiteley of Queensway, John Flew and William Henry Gibbs, as well as the Athenaeum Club and the Royal Library at Windsor. I have been unable to find the original publication price.

His manuscript was presented to Fulham Library with instructions as to its care and preservation, and it is still available to researchers who have the stamina to peruse its vast size and decipher Fèret's handwriting, which is clear enough until he begins altering or revising.

The collection of original illustrations was bought for £100 by William Hayes Fisher and presented to Fulham Library. Feret was doubtless pleased to receive the money, as the publication, far from enriching him in any way, left him out of pocket, he reckoned, by about £600.

Fulham Old and New received many appreciative and lengthy reviews, some of which add to Feret's own comments on the times and the changes they were bringing to his neighbourhood. The reviewer in *Notes and Queries*, for example, notes that the volumes confirmed that 'Fulham like the rest of London has suffered the processes of destruction which rage there and shows rows of squalid houses which are a reproach to our tastes and civilisation'. *Literature* said that Fèret's efforts were all the more commendable as Fulham lacked the literary and social savour of Hampstead, Chiswick, Chelsea and Richmond. This reviewer would not even concede that Fulham Palace made up for this shortcoming. 'As regard three of its fronts', he said, 'it is one of the ugliest and most depressing houses in England, a mere box of bricks peirced by windows.' 'Fulham is indeed fortunate in its historian' said one reviewer. 'If most of its historical sites have vanished the memory of them is preserved in this book with a fulness of detail and scrupulous accuracy.' *The Athenaeum* added 'The glory of Fulham has departed, it is well therefore that an industrious writer should give a complete history of its past repute.'

Certainly it is true that if Fèret had not undertaken his work at that time it is unlikely that anyone else would have been prepared to devote so long a period of their lives to the subject.

After his mother's death, Feret continued to live in Edith Road with his sister, Cordelia, until about 1897. He then moved to Churchfield Mansions in New King's Road and later to Hurlingham Road, although he appears to have kept the freehold of the Edith Road house, for it appears in his will. He left the *Fulham Chronicle* in 1901, and also left London, to take up a new career in Margate, selling antiques. He never married, but in 1894 adopted a 14-year-old girl, Lillie Darlington, from an orphanage known as Miss Sharman's. She was consumptive and committed suicide in 1917. Fèret afterwards adopted another daughter, Lilian White, whose mother moved in as his housekeeper. Lilian eventually gave much help to Michael Dewe when he was writing his invaluable little book on Fèret,[1] to which I am indebted for my information on this remarkable man, who though a household name among London historians, is unknown to the general public.

Fèret died in 1921, at the age of 66, of a heart attack during a bout of pneumonia, and is buried at Margate.

NOTES ON SOURCES

1   Michael Dewe, *Fulham's Historian, Charles Feret* (Fulham and Hammersmith Historical Society 1972).

Bibliography

AUBREY, John, *Brief Lives*, (Clarendon Press 1898)

BATES, L.M., *The Thames on Fire* (1985).

BLOMFIELD, Alfred, *Memoirs of Charles James Blomfield, Bishop of London*, (1863).

BOLITHO, H. and REED, D., *Without the City Wall* (1952).

BOWACK, John, *Antiquities of Middlesex*, Vol. II (1706).

BRACKEN, A.H., *Guide to Fulham Parish Church*, revised by Dennis Haselgrove (1973).

CARPENTER, Edward, *The Protestant Bishop* (1956).

CARPENTER, Spencer Cecil, *Winnington Ingram – a Biography* (1949).

CHAMBERS, R., (ed.) *Book of Days* (1863–4).

COLLINSON, Patrick, *Archbishop Grindal* (1979).

CROKER, Thomas Crofton, *A Walk from London to Fulham* (1860), originally published in *Fraser's Magazine*, 1845.

DENNY, Barbara, *King's Bishop* (1985).

DEWE, George and Michael, *Fulham Bridge 1729–1886* (1986).

DEWE, Michael, *Fulham's Historian – Charles Fèret* (1972).

Dictionary of National Biography.

DORLING, Captain Taprell ('Taffrail'), *The Hurlingham Club 1869–1953*, (1953).

FALLOWS, William Gordon, *Mandell Creighton and the English Church* (1964).

FAULKNER, Thomas, *An Historical and Topographical Account of Fulham* (1813).

FÈRET, Charles, *Fulham Old and New* (1900).

FITZGERALD, Percy, *London City Suburbs* (1893).

Fulham Chronicle files.

HADDON, R., (compiler) *Reminiscences of Prebendary Rogers, Rector of St Botolph's, Bishopsgate* (1887).

HAMMERSMITH AND FULHAM LIBRARIES, *How we used to travel* (1974).

HASKER, Leslie, *The Place which is called Fulanham* (1981).

HASKER, Leslie, *Fulham in the Second World War* (1984).

HUGHES, Bernard, *Victorian Pottery and Porcelain* (1959).

JENKINS, Simon, *Landlords to London* (1975).

LEFEBURE, Molly *Murder with a Difference* (1958).

LYSONS, Daniel, *Environs of London* (1796).

MURRAY, John J., *The Quest for the Golden Lion* (1981).

Peterborough School *Magazine*.

PURCELL, William, *Fisher of Lambeth* (1969).

STODDARD, Jeanne, *One hundred years of Sugar in Hammersmith 1874–1974* (1974).

STRYPE, John, *Survey of London* (1720).

STRYPE, John, *Life of Aylmer* (1701).

TREVOR-ROPER, Hugh *Archbishop Laud* (1962).

THORNBURY W., and WALFORD, E., *Old and New London* (1873).

WHITEHOUSE, Keith, *A Brief History of Fulham Palace* (1983).

WHITTING, P.D., (ed.), *History of Fulham* (1970).

WILLSON, E.J., *West London Nursery Gardens* (1982).

Appendix

HAMMERSMITH AND FULHAM ARCHIVES AND LOCAL HISTORY COLLECTIONS

The Archive and Local History collections are divided between three locations and you are advised to telephone in advance for an appointment.

For printed material about Fulham, photographs, prints, maps, books, newspapers, directories and voters' lists, ephemera, Fulham Local History Collection, Fulham Library, 589 Fulham Road, SW6 5NX (081–748 3020 *ext* 3875).

For archives and documents, including copies of the census returns for Hammersmith and Fulham 1841–1881 and general information about local history services in the borough, Hammersmith and Fulham Archives, Shepherds Bush Library, 7 Uxbridge Road, W12 8LJ (081–748 3020 *ext* 3850).

Photographs, drawings and prints. The archives and local history collections contain some photographs dating back to the 1850s, and include portraits of local dignitaries, royal visits, bomb damage, school groups, street parties, people at work, as well as a modern photographic survey of the borough.

Books and newspapers. There is a large reference collection of books on all aspects of Fulham and Hammersmith, as well as works by authors who have lived in the area. Sets of street directories exist from the late 19th century and back copies of local newspapers are available for consultation either in bound copies or on microfilm.

Documents. The main archive is the official record of the forerunners of the present London Borough of Hammersmith and Fulham from the 17th century, including the records of the vestries of the parishes and the Board of Works.

Maps. The earliest map showing the area in any detail dates from 1741 and good examples of all the important maps of the locality since then are available for consultation.

The Archive and Local History departments appreciate contributions from the public. They will copy your photographs and return the originals. They are also pleased to see records of local clubs, societies, etc. The departments produce a wide range of publications for sale at modest prices, including books of old photographs, postcards and prints.

THE FULHAM AND HAMMERSMITH HISTORICAL SOCIETY

This Society aims to foster and encourage the study of local history and archaeology – it holds meetings and visits. It also compiles and publishes historical material, usually in an annual publication. Recent contributions include *Medicine in Fulham, Fulham's Historian*, (a biography of Charles Fèret) and *Fulham Bridge*. Further details of the Society may be obtained from the Secretary, 56 Palewell Park, SW14 8JH.

THE HAMMERSMITH AND FULHAM AMENITY TRUST.

This was set up in 1982 to make the borough a brighter and greener place, and to create employment. Its work includes landscaping, tree planting, waste recycling and the improvement of church gardens and the riverside. Further details are available from their headquarters at Palingswick House, 241 King Street, W6 9LP (081–741 5811).

Index

Illustrations are indicated in bold
type